THE BASS
RAILWAY TRIPS

THE BASS RAILWAY TRIPS

Rod Pearson

The Breedon Books
Publishing Company
Derby

First published in Great Britain by
The Breedon Books Publishing Company Limited
44 Friar Gate, Derby DE1 1DA
1993

ISBN 1 873626 62 2

Printed and bound by Hillmans Printers, Frome, Somerset.
Cover printed by BDC Printing Services Ltd of Derby.

Contents

Acknowledgements
6

Introduction
7

The Value of Advertising
8

Burton upon Trent and Brewing
9

The First Bass Trip
19

The Biennial Trips, 1867 to 1881
25

The Annual Trips Begin
32

The Later Excursions
37

Liverpool and New Brighton
41

Blackpool
49

Great Yarmouth
55

Scarborough
62

Trips and Trippers
69

End of the Bass Trips
76

Acknowledgements

Assistance is gratefully acknowledged from the following sources: Staff of the Public Libraries at Blackpool, Brighton, Burton upon Trent, Liverpool, Great Yarmouth, Scarborough and Wolverhampton, at the University of Derby and at the Bass Museum of Brewing, Burton upon Trent; Mr A.T.Moss of the *Burton Daily Mail*; Mr G Nutt; Mr Ben Ward, a former employee of the Bass breweries, provided valuable help in checking factual information and offering valuable anecdotes about the Bass Trips. By a curious coincidence he was born on the day of the Liverpool Trip of 1908. He recounts the tale of his father, who was sent out of the house early in the morning, being hailed from the top of a passing Ashby tramcar en route for Burton Station and invited to join the Trip. He declined, saying that he had more important things to attend to on this occasion! Shortly afterwards, Ben was born.

Photographic Acknowledgements

Unless otherwise credited, all illustrations are from the collection of the Bass Museum of Brewing, Burton upon Trent. Pictures of the Bass Special trains are rare. Where possible, illustrations have been taken from the original Bass Trip handbooks, although authenticity sometimes compromises quality.

Additional sources of information

The Bass Museum has published reprints of the Bass Trip handbooks for Great Yarmouth 1893, the first proper handbook, Liverpool 1904, technically and artistically one of the most pleasing, and Scarborough 1914, the last handbook of all. Each repays careful study, yielding information about the places visited and the nature of the journeys involved, but also giving an insight into the effort which went into the organisation of the huge railway excursions.

Of particular value is the book of C.C.Owen, *The Greatest Brewery in the World, A History of Bass, Ratcliff & Gretton*, published by the Derbyshire Record Society, 1992. Further information about Burton, Bass and Brewing is available at the Bass Museum.

Introduction

DURING the second half of the nineteenth century railway excursions, which had been part of the scene since the opening of the Liverpool and Manchester line, were run by all the major brewing firms in the Staffordshire town of Burton upon Trent as an annual treat for their workforces. By far the largest of these brewery excursions were those organised by Messrs Bass, Ratcliff & Gretton, reflecting the importance of the company as a major employer and producer of beer in the town.

The 'Bass Railway Trips', as they became known, were not only the largest trips run from Burton but were, it was claimed by the organisers, some of the largest railway excursions organised by a private company anywhere in the world. As many as seventeen trains were used, and on one occasion more than 11,000 people were carried in a single day between Burton upon Trent and Blackpool. This book examines the rise and fall of the brewery railway excursion which was a feature of the social diary of Burton upon Trent for almost half a century prior to World War One.

The Value of Advertising

Bass Trips – newspaper reports

FOR several years the *Burton Daily Mail* published a special edition in the week following the Bass Trip containing their own account of the Trip and reprinting reports from other newspapers around the country. Some of these accounts were quite lengthy, others were merely a paragraph, but they are indicative of the interest which the Bass Excursions aroused by their very size.

The *Burton Daily Mail — Bass's Special Edition —* of Thursday, 29 July 1909, reported the trip to Yarmouth on Friday, 23rd. It also carried accounts from the following papers: *Morning Leader; Daily Dispatch; Manchester Courier; London Evening News; London Star; Daily Chronicle; Eastern Evening News; Nottingham Guardian; Evening Standard; Daily Telegraph; Daily Mail; Eastern Daily News; Birmingham Gazette and Express; Daily Sketch; Sheffield Telegraph; Reynold's Newspaper; Newcastle Journal.*

Other newspapers in whose pages the praises of the guidebook were sung were the *Manchester Courier, Blackpool Gazette, Blackpool Times, Railway Gazette, Railway Review, Midland Evening News, East Anglian Daily Times, Staffordshire Sentinel, Dundee Courier, North-Eastern Gazette* and *Middlesbrough Gazette.*

A Mug of "Bass"

A MUG of "Bass!" More clear and fine,
More bracing than the ripest wine.
The fragrance of the country air,
And yellow grain and meadows fair,
And grassy slopes with lowing kine,
And mellow warmth of rich sunshine,
All mingle in this draught divine.
Old Jove might quaff and Hebe bear
A mug of "Bass."

Served with a chop of South-Down line,
Or toasted trotters of the swine,
It brings a flavour deep and rare,
With which no scarlet lips compare:
Touch them who will: I press to mine
A mug of "Bass."

Great Yarmouth
Handbook, 1893.

Burton upon Trent and Brewing

FOR as long as anyone could remember, most towns in Britain had a small brewing industry, beer being produced in small ale-houses for consumption on the premises, and in this respect Burton upon Trent was no exception. Indeed it may be noted that up to the early eighteenth century, the neighbouring town of Derby had a larger output of malt and beer.

Along Burton's High Street in the late eighteenth century were to be found several small family concerns engaged in the production of modest amounts of beer, and it was from this small nucleus that there arose an industry which was to dominate the town and to make Burton nationally famous for the brewing of beer, as a result of a growing reputation for the quality of its brewing products, particularly through the small consignments which were reaching a discerning market in London.

The completion of improvements to the navigation along the River Trent in 1712 expanded the opportunities for the brewers of Burton by providing easier, faster and cheaper transport for their bulky products to the ports of Gainsborough and Kingston upon Hull. The way was now open for the transport of greater quantities of beers to the London market, using coastal shipping, and also to ports along the Baltic Sea coast, including St Petersburg, which was to stimulate a return trade in Memel oak and iron bars, both of which were required by the brewing and allied trades.

From the 1750s there was an expansion in the Burton brewing industry — although not significantly greater than in any other town — mainly as a result of the use of the clear, hard water from the wells beneath the town which resulted in a beer that could withstand the prolonged journey to the Baltic region without undue deterioration. The increased trade resulted in it outgrowing the traditional small brewhouses of families including Wilson,

The town that beer built! Framed in a barrel of Bass beer is this postcard view of Burton upon Trent from the south, taken about 1900. In the foreground is Stapenhill Cemetery. The skyline is dominated by the chimneys of several breweries, while the arches of Burton bridge can be seen on the right, crossing the floodplain of the River Trent. Most of the views in this section are from the early years of the twentieth century, when brewing and the railway trips were in their heyday.

The breweries seen from the river, Burton upon Trent. On the left are Worthington's maltings, now the site of the town Library; in the centre is the Bass Old Brewery with the water tower of 1866, the only surviving building in this scene, and to the right is Allsop's lager brewery. Smoke is rising from two locomotives in the Hay Sidings, which hold wagons of the Great Northern and Midland Railways.

Evans, Worthington, Clay and Bass, who began to invest in purpose-built breweries, to enable better quality control and to increase output.

William Bass first came to Burton in 1756 in connection with a highly profitable business as a carrier of general goods, including beer, between London and Manchester. He invested his profits in premises on the east side of High Street which included a brewhouse in 1777, and by his death in 1788 he had established a reputation as a brewer of good beer, supplying local innkeepers, merchants and innkeepers in Manchester and London, and merchants in Hull as well as direct to Baltic port customers. He was succeeded by his elder son, Michael, who went into partnership with Samuel Ratcliff (1809) and John Gretton (1835).

In common with the other Burton brewers, they were able to take advantage of the new Trent and Mersey Canal which, since its completion in 1777, had added a new dimension to the transport facilities of the area by giving waterway connections to both Liverpool and Bristol, in addition to the existing outlet to the Humber. The trade with the Baltic states was brought to an abrupt halt by the imposition of a sea blockade by the Napoleonic fleet in 1806, which resulted in the collapse of several of the smaller brewing firms. Although the trade resumed in 1815, it was to last only a further ten years. Some relief was found by exploiting new overseas markets through Liverpool and London, in particular with the export of India Pale Ale to the sub-continent and elsewhere in Britain's expanding

overseas possessions. Much of this trade was shared by the firms of Bass, Allsopp, Salt and Worthington.

When Michael Bass died in 1827, control of the firm passed to his son, Michael Thomas Bass (II), who was to form a partnership with Samuel Ratcliff and John Gretton. Bass, Ratcliff & Gretton, like the other large brewers in Burton, were becoming more efficient through concentrating on the brewing process using the Burton union system of fermentation and they were able and ready to respond to a major new challenge when the first railway through the town, the Birmingham and Derby Junction, opened in 1839.

Burton now had access to a fast and rapidly expanding transport system which would soon embrace much of the country from Cornwall to the North of Scotland. More immediately it gave easier access to the important London market and to the ports of London and Liverpool which accounted for a quarter of the firm's output. The growing trade was reflected in changes to the town of Burton, which saw the infilling of the area between the High Street and the railway with a complex of new industrial premises and housing.

The firm of Bass, Ratcliff & Gretton continued to grow at a faster rate than its competitors and by the end of the nineteenth century was operating four separate brewing premises in the town. The various sites were linked to each other and to the Midland Railway by a private railway system from the 1860s, which with sixteen miles of line and

The gates of the Bass New Brewery on Station Street, Burton, from the corner of George Street, about 1900. The chimneys are almost hidden by the clouds of vapour venting from the top of the buildings, a reminder of the sights, sounds and smells which pervaded the town. There were nineteen brewing companies in Burton at the beginning of the century, of which Bass, Ratcliff & Gretton was by far the largest in both employment and output. The excursions organised by the breweries offered a chance for employees to escape from the realities of their everyday lives for one day each year. The picture is by Richard Keene, a local photographer, who supplied many illustrations for the Bass Trip booklets.

The Bass wharves at Shobnall, with stacks of oak staves, many covered with sacking, for making beer casks. In the background is the large building and chimney of Grange Pumping Station on Shobnall Road, one of several underground sources of water for the Bass brewing processes. The men and their families and friends would be regular participants in the Bass Trips.

There are 101 men posed in this picture of Bass's steam cooperage in the Middle Yard. They were all good customers of the Bass special trains on Trip Days, and were carefully marshalled with their families into designated trains under the arrangements of William Walters. This building still survives and houses the Bass transport maintenance section.

Unloading empty casks for cleaning and repairing at the Shobnall storage banks. The open-sided storage areas were a bleak working environment in the winter months. Perhaps a free day at the seaside was a small compensation for the discomforts of the workplace.

The Burton Breweries were almost totally dependent upon the railways for their supplies of raw materials and the delivery of their final products away from Burton. Several breweries made extensive use of private sidings for the movement of materials and casks between their own premises. The largest system was operated by Bass, Ratcliff & Gretton; eight of their locomotives are seen, ready for a day's work, in this view of about 1910.

Station Street with trams. A postcard view of 1910. Tramcar No.13 has arrived from the direction of the railway station and is about to turn right towards the Branstone Road terminus. The overhead wiring is prominent in the picture but the publisher has removed the trolley pole from the tram! The street is still recognisable, although this section is now pedestrianised and the Wheat Sheaf Hotel has been converted into shops and offices.

Station Street with prams, looking towards its junction with High Street in 1910. The street has been watered to keep down the dust, no doubt appreciated by the ladies wheeling their perambulators and dressed in the fine outfits which would also make an appearance on the railway trips. A.T.Moss.

running powers over another ten miles of the mainline railway was the largest of the brewery lines in the town.

The Bass railway had its own fleet of locomotives to handle the internal traffic and to exchange several hundreds of wagons daily with the mainline railway. By the end of the century the Midland Railway had become noted as a carrier of both coal and beer, with London as a major market for both items. The Midland main line through Leicester was eventually quadrupled to carry the coal traffic, while the platforms of St Pancras Station (1868) were supported by vaulted cellars built to dimensions suitable for the storage of barrels of beer from Burton.

It has been calculated by C.C.Owen that in 1888 the various Burton breweries employed a total of 8,215 people, of whom just over one-third were employed by the single firm of Bass, Ratcliff & Gretton. By this time the population of the town was about 45,000 and it is quite clear that most families in the town had some employment connection with the brewing industry and with one firm in particular, which would be reflected in the size of railway excursions organised by Bass, Ratcliff & Gretton.

It was the practice of many of the larger brewers to use some of their profits for gifts, often in the form of public buildings or similar facilities, to the citizens of the towns which had created their wealth. Michael Thomas Bass (II) made several such gifts to Burton during his lifetime, including the church of St Paul, which was consecrated in 1874, and an institute for the church in St Paul's Street East. He was succeeded in 1884 by his son, Michael Arthur Bass, who was to be created Baron Burton in 1886. The public gifts continued, in the form of a new institute for St Paul's in 1892, enabling him to present the earlier building to the Borough of Burton as its new Town Hall in 1894. Other firms made gifts to their workforce in the form of Christmas parties and other treats, including outings and railway excursions. In this respect the firm of Bass was something of a laggard, holding its first trip in 1865. But it soon outstripped its rivals in the scale and complexity of its works' outings.

Railway Excursions

By the 1860s, railway excursions had become a commonplace event, enabling the poorer paid members of the working classes to escape from their everyday drudgery for a few hours of pleasure and relaxation. Within the span of a single generation an insular society had been changed into one which accepted long-distance travel as a normal event. From their early days the railway companies realised that there was profit to be made from the moving of large numbers of people and that cheap tickets produced full trains. Thomas Cook of Melbourne, Derbyshire, is usually credited with initiating the idea of excursions with his trip for Temperance enthusiasts from Leicester to Loughborough on 5 July 1841, but he was

High Street by the Market Place, Burton upon Trent, seen at a remarkably quiet moment in about 1910. On Trip days the streets would be thronged in the early hours by excursionists making their way to and from the special trains. Each year appeals were made for a quiet and orderly return home! The large building on the right still remains, but that on the left has been cleared for the access to Burton Shopping Centre along St Modwen's Walk.   A.T.Moss.

The view along Horninglow Street towards the Burton bridge in about 1906, at the junction with Guild Street from where the Corporation tramway emerged on the route to Winshill. Passengers for the Bass Trips who lived in the area were aroused in the early hours by the sound of bugles in the streets. Now only the Plough Inn (no longer an inn) and the third block of two small shops on the right beyond Guild Street remain. Everything else has gone, including the large church of Holy Trinity, its congregation dispersed elsewhere by urban redevelopment. The entrance to Guild Street has been widened and the car park of the Bass Museum has replaced the shops on the right.   A.T.Moss.

Worthington's level crossing with its signal box in High Street in 1910. On the left of the crossing is the office of Thoday and Son, Barley Merchants, and on the right are the shops formerly occupied by Barratt and Son, gun makers and surgical instrument and cycle dealers. Then comes the old Blue Posts Inn, followed by the confectioner's shop of Mrs H.Keen and then the offices of Mr William Small, solicitor and commissioner for oaths and of Mr J.H.Talbot, solicitor. The quietness of the scene and the smart dress of passers-by suggests that the picture was taken on a summer Sunday. The Blue Posts Inn has been rebuilt and Worthington Way occupies the site of the level crossing and signal box.
A.T.Moss

applying an established principle, the difference being that he was acting as an individual travel agent at his own financial risk. Within a short time he was planning, and successfully running, excursions for pleasure, the first being a trip to Liverpool and Snowdonia in 1845. It was the Great Exhibition of 1851 which brought out the best in Cook's abilities when, despite the reluctance of the Midland Railway, he organised the visit of

165,000 visitors to London. Other railway companies carried people from all over Britain to London for the Exhibition and this event helped to fix the idea of excursions by rail firmly in the public mind.

It was the railway which popularised and vulgarised the seaside resorts of Britain, transforming the nature of the clientele in some cases, such as Brighton, enhancing the already established reputation of others, like Southend,

The brewing industry of Burton was able to grow because of early improvements to the Trent navigation but especially with the arrival of the railway in 1839. Here the two have come together in the floods of August 1912; a Worthington locomotive propels a few wagons, one containing empty casks, through the Hay Sidings in front of Allsopp's lager brewery.

and leading to some wholly new creations of the railway age, notably Blackpool and Skegness. In most instances the popular appeal of the seaside resorts was the mixture of sun, sand, scenery, plenty of entertainment, feeding facilities for the masses and somewhere to shelter if the weather should turn wet or cold, and it was these resources which were exploited by the railway companies in their continuing quest for profit until the time when motor transport began to carry trippers to their destinations.

It was common practice for many private industrial firms to organise excursions for their employees and where there was rivalry between local firms, the treats for employees could assume great significance. It was to be expected that in Burton upon Trent the existence of so many firms in the same industry would generate much comment, the local newspapers referring to the summer months as the 'Trips Season'.

The Bass Trips

The Bass Trips started in a modest way in 1865, but under the guidance of William Walters, the Bass traffic manager, they came to outstrip those of the rival breweries in both size and complexity of operations. At first the Bass Trips were held every two years, but from 1883 they became an annual event eagerly anticipated by the company's employees. William Walters organised the Trips with military-style precision, producing in the later years a series of comprehensive, illustrated guides which were issued to all participants.

The railway excursions fulfilled several purposes. They were an important source of advertising for the brewing company, the sheer size of the undertaking attracting considerable attention both at home and abroad. They were regarded by the firm as treats for the workforce, but were in reality a form of profit sharing on a modest scale. In addition to the immediate pleasures of a day trip there were also longer term advantages to be found in the education of the workers. Some of the earlier Trips coincided with major industrial and cultural exhibitions while in the later years music and the arts were among the entertainments laid on at the resorts, events that were well-patronised by the trippers. Another motive from the company point of view was the need to keep the employees happy and contented, to try to avoid industrial strife and loss of production which might occur with a

Early transport in Burton. The ferry across the River Trent at Stapenhill, before the building of the Ferry Bridge and viaduct in 1889, which gave a footway clear of the river floods and enabled the development of suburban housing to the south of the river. The bridge was one of many gifts to the town by Lord Burton and was freed of tolls by the Town Corporation in 1898. A.T.Moss.

disaffected labour force. In this respect Messrs. Bass, Ratcliff & Gretton were no different to other firms throughout the length and breadth of Britain. Each social group in the workforce was firmly segregated, even in the ordering of places on the excursion trains, while the patronising tone of the instructions, issued

with the best of intentions of Mr Walters, would today be quite unacceptable.

World War One brought the Bass Trips to an end, the last being held just a few days before war broke out. Over the years more than a quarter of a million trippers were carried and it is a remarkable fact that in all these Trips

Table 1.
The Bass Trips

Year	Date	Day	Destination	Trains	Passengers	Year	Date	Day	Destination	Trains	Passengers
1865	19 August	Sat	Liverpool	2	1,000	1893	16 June	Fri	Yarmouth	15	8,000
1867	24 August	Sat	Crystal Palace	2	1,000	1894	15 June	Fri	Scarborough	15	8,000
1869	14 August	Sat	London	3	1,500	1895	14 June	Fri	Liverpool	15	8,000
1871	24 June	Sat	London	3	1,800	1896	12 June	Fri	Blackpool	16	10,000
1873	5 July	Sat	Liverpool	1	900	1897	11 June	Fri	Yarmouth	15	8,500
			London	3	1,600	1898	17 June	Fri	Scarborough	15	9,000
1875	25 June	Fri	Crystal Palace	3		1899	16 June	Fri	Liverpool	16	10,000
			London	1	3,000	1900	15 June	Fri	Blackpool	17	11,241
1877	22 June	Fri	Liverpool	4	2,650	1901	14 June	Fri	Yarmouth	16	10,000
			Manchester	1	650	1902	11 July	Fri	Scarborough	16	8,000
1879	13 June	Fri	London	6	3,100	1903	17 July	Fri	Blackpool	17	9,800
1881	17 June	Fri	Scarborough	6	3,500	1904	15 July	Fri	Liverpool	17	9,000
1883	15 June	Fri	London	6	3,500	1905	14 July	Fri	Yarmouth	16	8,000
1884	30 August	Sat	Wolverhampton	5	3,000	1906	20 July	Fri	Scarborough	16	8,000
1885	19 June	Fri	Blackpool	8	4,000	1907	19 July	Fri	Blackpool	17	10,000
1886	11 June	Fri	London	8	4,000	1908	17 July	Fri	Liverpool	15	8,000
1887	17 June	Fri	Liverpool	8	4,500	1909	23 July	Fri	Yarmouth	15	9,000
1888	15 June	Fri	Brighton	10	4,500	1910	22 July	Fri	Scarborough	15	8,000
1889	21 June	Fri	Blackpool	11	5,000	1911	21 July	Fri	Blackpool	15	8,000
1890	15 August	Fri	Scarborough	13	6,000	1912	19 July	Fri	Liverpool	14	7,000
1891	14 August	Fri	Liverpool	13	6,300	1913	25 July	Fri	Yarmouth	14	7,000
1892	17 June	Fri	Blackpool	15	7,500	1914	24 July	Fri	Scarborough	14	8,000

Passenger figures are approximate.
Sources: *Burton Weekly News* and *General Advertiser* and *Burton Daily Mail*, held at Central Library, Burton upon Trent, Staffordshire. Also individual railway excursion booklets — Bass Museum.

Road transport available for hire, manufactured in Burton upon Trent. A small omnibus with seats for twelve, built by the Ryknield Car Company of Shobnall Road, outside the Bell Hotel in Horninglow Street. Note the solid tyres and simple springing.   A.T.Moss.

Another product of the Ryknield Car Company. The pneumatic tyres, the sumptuous leather upholstery, and the chain drive to the rear wheel can be clearly seen.   A.T.Moss.

there were only two fatal accidents, one of these occurring on the actual rail journey. London was a popular choice for the earlier excursions, but in later years the size of the Trips dictated a cycle of destinations to the major resorts of Yarmouth, Scarborough, Blackpool and Liverpool (for New Brighton).

This account includes a complete list of the Bass Trips (*Table 1*) and draws its information from the archives held at the Bass Museum of Brewing and from contemporary reports published by the newspapers in Burton and the resort towns visited. In addition, surviving copies of the handbooks published by William Walters provide a valuable insight into the

degree of organisation essential for the smooth running of the monster excursions.

Many of the Bass trains arrived home in the early hours of the morning, prompting Mr Walters to appeal for a quiet return home through the streets of the sleeping town. He never failed to remind his readers of the generosity of the company's directors in providing the outing for workers and their families. Notwithstanding the best efforts of the Midland Railway, he also offered thanks to the Almighty for mercifully preserving the whole undertaking during the many years in which the Bass Trips had run.

The First Bass Trip

ON SATURDAY 19 August 1865, two special trains, carrying just over one thousand people, all employees of Messrs Bass, Ratcliff & Gretton, left Burton upon Trent at about 6am for a day excursion to Liverpool. This seemed an unlikely choice of destination, but it reflected the strong connections which the brewing firm had with the port, through which much of its export trade was shipped. The train journey, which was rather long and tedious, started on the North Staffordshire line to Crewe, thence over the L&NWR line to Lime Street Station, Liverpool.

Tickets for the trip were issued to workmen only. Wives and sweethearts were not invited, which was perhaps fortunate, because the trains were stuck for about an hour in Edge Hill tunnel on the approach to Liverpool. In those days it was the practice to detach the railway engines at Edge Hill and work the carriages into the station on a rope haulage. The delay, in the semi-darkness and in a suffocating, sulphurous atmosphere, gave the excursionists what was later described as a 'lively and enjoyable time.' The trains finally arrived in Lime Street station at 11am, taking five hours for a trip which should have been little more than four.

In Liverpool, a cruise on the Mersey had been organised for the party. It was intended to march in a procession through the streets to the Pier Head and the men lined up behind the Burton Volunteer Band. Unfortunately, the effect was spoiled by the police, who refused the band permission to play in the streets. At the Pier Head, two specially chartered steamboats, the *Universe* and the *Constitution*, were waiting for a trip which took the party up-river on the Liverpool side, providing a view of the docks and shipping, before crossing to Eastham on the Cheshire bank. From there the two boats, sailing in close company, moved downstream to the North West lighthouse, passing close to the Birkenhead docks and the New Brighton Fort, before returning to the city waterfront.

After what was described in the *Burton on*

Mr Michael Arthur Bass MP, the great-grandson of the founder of the brewing firm, who hosted the dinner for the men on the first Bass trip to Liverpool, in 1865. He became a baronet in 1882 and a baron in 1886; as Lord Burton he continued to actively encourage the running of the Bass Trips until his death in 1909.

Trent Times of Saturday, 26 August 1865 as 'an agreeable and pleasant ride', the party was ready to enjoy a dinner starting at 4pm at the Corn Exchange, Brunswick Street. The *Liverpool Mercury* noted that the Exchange was decorated with various banners, whose slogans read, "Welcome to Liverpool", "May Agriculture and Commerce ever Flourish",

BASS & CO'S.
TRIP TO LIVERPOOL.
AUGUST 19th, 1865.

RULES
To be observed during the day by their Workmen.

No. 1.--The men belonging to the Old, Middle, and New Breweries, Carpenters Building, Fitters', Painters', Wheelwrights', Waggoners' & Labourers departments, will assemble at the Burton Railway Station, precisely **at a quarter before 6 o'clock, a.m.,** on Saturday next, and enter **No. 1** SPECIAL TRAIN, under the direction of their foremen, as follows, viz., Old Brewery 1st., Middle Brewery 2nd., and New Brewery 3rd, Carpenters 4th., Building 5th., Fitters 6th., Painters, Wheelwrights, Waggoners 7th., and Labourers, &c., &c., according to the labels on the Carriages.

No. 2.--The men belonging to the Railway Maltster's, New Stores, Smith's, Middle Yard, and Cooper's Departments, will assemble at the Burton Railway Station, **precisely at 6 o'clock, a.m.,** on Saturday next, and enter **No. 2** SPECIAL TRAIN, under the direction of their foremen, as follows, Railway 1st., Maltsters 2nd., New Stores 3rd., Smiths 4th., Middle Yard 5th., Coopers, &c, &c., according to the labels on the Carriages.

No. 3.--The Trains will stop for five minutes at Crewe going and returning, and it is requested the men will not go into the Refreshment Rooms in a body but make arrangements with their foremen on the Platform to get them what they may require.

No. 4. It is also particularly requested that no man will leave or enter the train when in motion, or leave the train at Edge-hill Station, Liverpool.

No. 5.--Train **No. 1** will arrive at Lime-street Station, Liverpool, about 10 a.m., when those who wish to embark on board the " UNIVERSE" Steam boat, will proceed at once to Prince,s Landing Stage.

No. 6.--Train **No. 2** will arrive at Lime-street Station, Liverpool, about 10.20 a.m., when those who wish to embark on board the "CONSTITUTION" Steam boat, will proceed at once to Prince's Landing Stage.

No. 7.--The dinner will take place in the Corn Exchange, Brunswick-street, Liverpool, at **4 p m.** and it is requested the men will enter the room in an orderly manner, viz., the Old Brewery men. 1st., Middle Brewery 2nd., New Brewery 3rd., and so on in rotation as they entered the trains. The dinner tickets then to be given to the collectors.

No. 8.--Train **No. 1** will return to Burton from Lime-street Station at a quarter before **8 p.m.,** and it is requested that all the men belonging to that train will assemble on the Platform at half-past **7 o'clock, p.m.,** and enter the same carriages as when leaving Burton.

No. 9.--Train **No. 2** will return to Burton from Lime-street at **8.15, p.m.** and it is requested all the men belonging to that train will assemble on the Platform at a quarter before **8 o'clock p.m.,** and enter the same carriages as when leaving Burton.

No. 10.--Heads of departments will see that the above instructions are carried out in a firm and courteous manner.

Burton-on-Trent,
   August 16th, 1865.

BASS, RATCLIFF, & GRETTON.

WHITEHURST, PRINTER BY STEAM-POWER, BURTON-ON-TRENT.

Each man on the first Bass Trip to Liverpool, in 1865, was issued with a set of rules drawn up by Captain Anderson of the Bass Engineers' Department. The meticulous attention to detail was a characteristic feature of all the Bass Trips.

Tickets for the first Bass Trip gave admission to the dinner held in the Corn Exchange, Liverpool.

"May the Sun never cease to shine on the Queen's Dominions" and "Health, Wealth and Prosperity to our respected employers, Messrs Bass, Ratcliff and Gretton." So the scene was set for an excellent repast, with Mr Michael Arthur Bass, MP presiding over a series of toasts and speeches of varying length and tedium.

Responding to a toast to the health of the brewing company, Mr Bass spoke at length on the duties of a firm to its employees. He said that he was really quite ashamed that this was the first excursion which has been made by the firm, but he promised that there would be more in the future, the remark being received with loud applause from his audience. Mr Bass concluded his speech with some further

observations on the benefits of good industrial relations. After more toasts and responses, the band played the National Anthem, whereupon the company dispersed and the excursionists made their way back to the railway station. The trains departed from Liverpool at about 8pm, arriving in Burton in the early hours of Sunday morning. The length of the speeches must have been something of an ordeal for the excursionists, leaving them with very little time to explore the delights of Liverpool. This was put right on the next excursion two years hence, when the formal dinner for the men was dispensed with, being replaced by a gratuity in lieu, which became the practice continued on all the succeeding Bass Trips.

The arrangements for the first Bass Trip to Liverpool were made by Capt J.W.Anderson of the Engineers' Department at the brewery. The men's instructions for the visit were issued on a folded two-page sheet, showing a degree of organisation which reflected his military background. Responsibility for the excursions was transferred to the Bass traffic department in time for the second trip in 1867. Anderson had joined Messrs Bass, Ratcliff and Gretton as a manager in 1855, following military service in India and most recently the post of Superintendent of Police in Burton. He moved within the company from the Engineers' Department to the Steam Cooperage Office. Although Anderson took no further part in the

Princes landing stage, Liverpool, with an unidentified paddle steamer. The first Bass Trip included a sail on the Mersey in specially chartered boats. Over the years many thousands of Bass Trippers enjoyed free cruises on the Mersey ferries to New Brighton. Trips out to sea, including visits to North Wales and the Isle of Man, could also be purchased at cheap rates.

A remarkable collection of whiskers! A visit to the Bass brewery by Agency officials and customers, in the early 1900s. Valued friends and customers of the firm were invited to participate as guests on the firm's railway trips, and were treated to dinners hosted by Mr Walters at the resorts. Special connecting services and, in later years, complete trains were arranged for the conveyance of Agency Staff to join the main excursion.

Another tour of inspection of the Bass brewery premises. Seats have been installed in a specially cleaned Midland Railway wagon, which also carries a ladder for use if a suitable wharf or platform is not available. Some of the party are posed on the locomotive. Standing third from left at the back of the wagon is William Walters, the Bass Traffic Manager and organiser of the company's railway trips.

Bass Trips, his subsequent career has a bearing on one of the later excursions. He fell seriously ill with a bronchial complaint and was sent on leave to the Mediterranean, where he recovered. On his return he was appointed Head of the Bass Agency in Brighton in 1881 and it is no coincidence that there was an excursion to the south coast resort in 1888.

As a footnote to the 1865 excursion, the following report was carried in the *Burton on Trent Times* on Saturday, 26 August 1865:
"Burton Petty Sessions: William Lee, labourer in the employ of Messrs Bass & Co, was charged with assaulting Police Constable Dale on Sunday night last, in High Street. It appeared from the evidence that the defendant was left behind in Liverpool by the excursion on Saturday, and did not return to Burton until Sunday evening. He was seen talking loudly and when asked to stop struck the Constable and was accordingly locked up. Fines of 5/- (*25p*) and 10/4d (*52p*); in default 14 days in prison.''

William Walters joins the Staff

William Walters was twenty-three years old when he joined the staff of the Traffic Department of Messrs Bass, Ratcliff & Gretton in 1865. He served as assistant to the Traffic Manager, John Cosgrove, who in later years was in poor health, being absent from the department through illness from 1880 until his death in 1883. Walters succeeded to the managership and proved ideally suited for the job, being a keen railway enthusiast, with a passion for anything to do with railway workings. He travelled extensively over the country on the various main lines, where he was a familiar figure. This interest is reflected in the amount of detail which his excursion booklets devoted to descriptions of the railway operation and equipment associated with the Bass Trips.

The transfer of responsibility for the second railway excursion to the Traffic Department gave Mr Walters an ideal opportunity to display his organisational ability. In later years he was assisted by Mr T.J.Lyle (from 1878) and Mr F.J.Eley (from 1884), whose efforts he always remembered to acknowledge. It is probable that these two carried out much of the local arrangements at the resorts selected to receive the Trips, but inevitably it was Mr Walters who attracted the tributes at dinners held for guests of the company on the Trips, where his efforts were lavishly praised and he was variously compared to the Admirable Crichton, the Kaiser Wilhelm and Napoleon!

On Trip days William Walters invariably sported an orchid buttonhole, the bloom being supplied by Mr Nisbet, the Head Gardener at the Bass home at Byrkley. Mr Walters would

Nothing was left to chance. To prevent the circulation of rumours in Burton concerning disasters which might have befallen the Bass special trains, Mr Walters made a practice of announcing their safe arrival with telegrams which were displayed at the brewery gates in Burton. This example is from the Liverpool Trip of 1904. Similar telegrams were sent at the end of the day to the various station masters at the resorts visited to tell of the safe arrival back in Burton.

Mr William Walters: He became Bass Traffic Manager in 1883 and retired in 1915, after 50 years of service with the Company. In 1867 he assumed responsibility for the Bass Trips, which he continued to organise until the last Trip in 1914.

send a carriage to Byrkley to collect the Nisbet family and bring them to Burton Station, where he received the orchid. He would then escort Nisbet, his wife and sons to a reserved compartment on their train.

It was the practice of Mr Walters to send a telegram to Burton announcing the safe arrival of the Bass Special trains at their destination. The telegram was affixed to the main brewery gates to allay any worries which relatives might have. In the handbooks he advised them to ignore any malicious rumours which might circulate prior to the arrival of his message. At the completion of the homeward journey he would likewise telegraph the news of the successful return of the Trip to the Stationmasters and other authorities which had hosted them for the day. Leaving nothing to chance Mr Walters also telegraphed the Meteorological Office for a weather forecast on Trip days. It is said that on one occasion, having received a forecast for Blackpool saying, "South-westerly winds, very showery," he refused to accept the forecast and telegraphed back saying, "We MUST have better weather!"

The Biennial Trips, 1867-1881

MR BASS was able to honour his public promise which he had made at Liverpool in 1865 by arranging for a second excursion two years later. With the approval of Mr Gretton he gave the responsibility of the organisation to William Walters. The venue selected was the Crystal Palace, which in 1854 had been rebuilt at Sydenham, in south-east London, where it became the principal facility in what the twentieth century would call a leisure complex. It was a favourite haunt for Victorian family outings, with gardens and fountains, exhibitions of natural history and the arts, and firework displays. The main building offered protection against the weather for large numbers of people and so offered an ideal combination of facilities similar to those at the seaside resorts chosen for later excursions.

The second Bass Trip was held on Saturday, 24 August 1867. This time the Trip was extended to clerks and some of their families. The *Burton Weekly News and General Advertiser* commented that from the early hours of the morning the streets of Burton had been astir with men and women, all making their

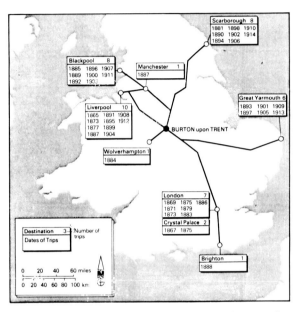

Map showing the destinations, routes and dates of the Bass Trips from 1865 to 1914. The Trips were run on forty-four occasions, biennially until 1883 and then every year until 1914. On three years there were visits to two destinations. The direct route from Burton to Liverpool was used in 1865; subsequent trips to Liverpool and Blackpool took the Midland line to Manchester through the Peak District of Derbyshire.

The Crystal Palace, visited by the Bass Trips in 1867 and 1875. The huge iron and glass building, built to a design by Joseph Paxton, originally accommodated the Great Exhibition in Hyde Park in 1851. It was reopened on its hilltop site at Sydenham in 1854. On the eastern side of the building, seen here, the slopes were lined with terraces, parkland, gardens and sports facilities. Twin water towers, designed by Mr I.K.Brunel, provided pressure for the ornamental fountains. Greater London Photograph Library.

The Crystal Palace was the forerunner of the modern leisure centre. The scale of the building can be judged from this view of indoor gardens and fountains. It was a popular venue for permanent and temporary displays, concerts and recitals.   Greater London Photograph Library.

way to one rendezvous — the railway station. Two trains were hired, carrying about one thousand excursionists. Mr Walters drew up a set of nine rules to be observed during the day, closely modelled on those for the Liverpool trip. The rules gave precise instructions about the way the men would enter the trains and the times at which these would depart. Rule

No.3 stated that the trains would arrive at Crystal Palace at 9.45am and 9.55am, although it would seem that this particular rule was beyond the control of Mr Walters. The rules also requested that during the journeys the men should not leave their carriages whilst in motion or go in a body to the refreshment rooms, but make arrangements with one of the

BASS & CO.'s TRIP

TO THE
CRYSTAL PALACE,
AUGUST 24TH, 1867.

RULES
TO BE OBSERVED BY THEIR WORKMEN DURING THE DAY.

No. 1.—The men belonging the Old, Middle, and New Breweries,—Railway, Carpenters, Joiners, Bricklayers, Building, Fitters and Engineers, Wheelwrights, Saw Mill and Waggoners Departments,—will assemble at the Burton Midland Railway Station, at the place marked No. 1 Special Train, Bass & Co.'s, precisely at 4 o'clock a.m., on Saturday next, and enter No. 1 SPECIAL under the direction of their Foremen, at 4-15 a.m., according to the labels on the carriages, as above stated, viz, Old Brewery first, &c, &c.

No. 2.—The men belonging to the Maltsters, Coopers, Stores, Smiths, Coppersmiths, Plumbers, Painters, Middle Yard, Watchmen, Labourers and Supernumeraries, will assemble at the Burton Midland Railway Station, at the place marked No. 2 Special Train, Bass & Co.'s, precisely at 4.15 a.m., on Saturday next, and enter No. 2 SPECIAL at 4-25 a.m., under the direction of their foremen, according to the labels on the carriages as above stated, viz, Maltsters first, &c., &c.

No. 3.—The trains will arrive at the Crystal Palace about 9.45 and 9-55 a.m., and it is particularly requested, going and returning, the men will not leave their carriages when in motion, or go in a body to the Refreshment Rooms, but make arrangements with one of their party in the carriage to get them what they require.

No. 4.—The Men are requested to be quiet and orderly, and assist the Foremen in carrying out their duties, to conform to the Rules and Regulations as posted up in the Crystal Palace, and to obey the instructions of the appointed Officers on duty.

No. 5.—Train No. 1 will leave the Crystal Palace about 6 p.m., as per Notices.

No. 6.—Train No. 2 will leave the Crystal Palace about 6-10 p.m., as per Notices.

No. 7.—The same order in entering the trains must be observed by the men of the various departments, when leaving the Crystal Palace, as at Burton Station.

No. 8.—Heads of Departments will please see that the above instructions are carried out in a firm and courteous manner, and keep their men well together when entering and leaving the trains.

No. 9.—Any Enquiry or Complaint to make, see Mr. W. WALTERS

BASS, RATCLIFF, & GRETTON.

Burton-on-Trent, August 20th, 1867.

R. R. BELLAMY. Machine Printer, 'Weekly News' oa, Burton-on-Trent

Rules for the guidance of participants on the Bass Trip to the Crystal Palace in 1867. This was the second trip and the first to be organised by William Walters. The rules are similar to those of the 1865 visit, and their echoes can be detected throughout succeeding years.

party in their carriage to get them what they required. Finally, any enquiries or complaints were to be directed to Mr Walters.

The trains left Burton in close succession at about 5am. The route took them southwards through Rugby and Kensington and after a journey of about five hours they reached the Crystal Palace Station. This was the first time that almost any of the excursionists had seen the famous glass and iron building. *The Burton Weekly News* said that 'they looked with an air of astonishment on the many wonderful objects that were to be seen at the Palace'. Equally impressive was the singing of a choir of 4,500 voices, which contributed to the sense of occasion. The return trains started back at 6pm and 6.10pm, reaching Burton soon after midnight.

By the time of the next Bass Trip, held in 1869, there were signs that the size of the undertaking was increasing. As yet, the Bass Trips were no more remarkable than those organised by other breweries in Burton upon Trent, but the continuing growth of the company in numbers of employees and output was reflected in the increasing size of the Trips, which by the end of the century far outstripped any others which originated in the town.

A fire on the night of 30 November 1936 destroyed the Crystal Palace. This aerial view shows the extent of the damage shortly after the blaze. The Bass trains would have used the High Level Station, seen here complete with turntable. There was a subway connection directly into the Palace. The station was opened in 1865 and demolished in 1954. The water towers were removed in 1942 to prevent their use as a landmark by German bombers.

Greater London Photograph Library.

London Bridge, looking towards Southwark, shortly after its widening in 1903-04.   Author's collection.

London was the destination for 1869 and on Saturday, 14 August three trains set out for London over the Midland route. The first train terminated at St Pancras, opened the previous year, whilst the other two ran into Ludgate Hill Station. For the majority of the excursionists the main attraction was a boat trip on the Thames, on one of several boats which sailed from St Paul's Pier for a voyage to North Woolwich where, according to the *Burton on Trent Times*, 'they resorted to the public gardens and enjoyed themselves as best they could'.

The return passage upstream enabled the excursionists to view the river frontage of the Houses of Parliament, before they landed at Westminster Pier. The remainder of the day was spent in sightseeing in the city before the return journey. This must have started quite late, as the last train arrived back in Burton at about 2.30am on Sunday.

Not all the trippers returned home that day. About 250 of them remained in London until Monday evening, 'passing their time away in one uninterrupted source of enjoyment and sight-seeing,' according to a report in the *Burton on Trent Times*. Whatever the excursionists might have got up to in London is not recorded, but the significance of their extra time in the city lies in the fact that an arrangement had been made with the Midland Railway Company to carry them home on a regularly scheduled service. This was a practice which became commonly associated with the Bass Trips, when those who could afford the time and expense of a few extra days away were provided with extension tickets to cover their return journey. These arrangements became quite elaborate for the larger excursions of later years.

In 1871 the first of several Bass Trips designed to coincide with major exhibitions was run, again to London. Three trains carried about 1,800 people, who were treated not only to the train journey but also to free admission to the International Exhibition. By now the principle of a gratuity was well-established, each man receiving half-a-crown (*12½p*) for the purposes of refreshments during the day. Once again an early start was made, the trains leaving Burton at 4.15am, 4.30am and 4.45am. The return from St Pancras was after the departure of the night mails. The last train arrived home at 2.30am on Sunday morning. Whether any extension tickets were granted on this occasion is not recorded, but all the other characteristics of the Bass railway trips had been well-established — good organisation and the skilful marshalling of hundreds of participants, a programme of events or entertainments throughout the day, including exhibitions designed to bring an element of culture into the proceedings. Very early starts and late finishes enabled the greatest possible value to be packed into the day, although the excursions must have made great demands upon the stamina of the participants.

The Bass Trip for 1873 was divided between two destinations, requiring the use of four trains. On Saturday, 5 July some 1,600 people went to London while 900 went to Liverpool. Each workman received a gratuity of 2s 6d (*12½p*), but those persons employed in the office

Liverpool Central Station, run by the Cheshire Lines Committee, became the regular station used by the Bass Specials to Liverpool and New Brighton. Limited platform facilities meant that smart work was needed to remove empty stock in the ten-minute interval between the arrival of trains.

Scarborough made its early reputation as a spa, which it attempted to preserve, as this postcard of 1905 suggests. But the majority of trippers were more interested in the sands, sunshine and entertainment which the commercial resort could offer.   Author's collection.

received five shillings (*25p*) and a first-class seat on the trains. The main body of the excursionists arrived back in Burton about 2am on Sunday. This was an unpopular timing. In 1875, the Trip was moved to a Friday, which was to remain the pattern for all future

Bass excursions. This change turned the occasion into a proper full-day holiday from work, but in order to avoid disadvantaging the lower-paid workers the bonus of a day's wages was added to the gratuity in future years, a gesture almost guaranteed to enhance the

The Bass Trips made their first of eight visits to Scarborough in 1881. The weather was not always kind to the trippers, as can be seen in this photograph of the gardens overlooking the North Bay. The flag gives an indication of wind strength on this rather dull day.

popularity of the Trips amongst the workforce. The move also meant that the early hours of the Sabbath day were no longer disturbed by homecoming roisterers, always a source of annoyance to attenders of church and chapel, particularly in view of the bugle notes which had echoed through the streets of Burton before dawn on the previous day, arousing both the trippers and anyone else within earshot.

The 1875 Trip involved three Bass trains to the Crystal Palace, with a fourth train going to St Pancras, the excursionists being provided with instructions how to reach various places of interest in the city. The total numbers of trippers reached three thousand on this occasion. The destinations for the 1877 Bass Trip were again split, but this time between Liverpool (four trains with 2,650 people) and Manchester (one train with 650 trippers). The Manchester trippers were given free admission into Belle Vue Gardens, where the attractions included a large firework display. The return train started from Belle Vue Station at 11.05pm.

and because of delays finally arrived in Burton at 3am. The first three trains from Liverpool returned to Burton uneventfully, arriving home at 12.25am, 1am and 1.15am, taking about four and a quarter hours. However, the final train, which left Liverpool at 8.50pm, was less fortunate. On reaching New Mills the engine broke down and was shunted into a siding. After considerable delay another engine was detached from a passing goods train and the excursion finally arrived back in Burton at 3.20am on Saturday morning. If the pattern of later years had been established by now, this train would have carried Mr Walters and his guests and he would not have been particularly amused.

In 1877 extension tickets were issued to 250 Liverpool trippers, most of whom took the opportunity to visit the Isle of Man, making the sea trip at their own expense. Charles Hanson, a clerk in the High Street office, took his family on the Trip to Liverpool and went on to Douglas. His son, then a lad of six years, later recounted that he had found difficulty in trying to swim in the recently opened Burton Baths (a gift to the town from the Ratcliff family) but found buoyancy and confidence in the salt water at Douglas. He returned home able to swim.

In 1879 six trains carried 3,100 excursionists to London, which should also have been the venue for 1881. However, an outbreak of smallpox in the capital caused the Directors to seek an alternative destination. The choice fell on the Yorkshire seaside resort of Scarborough. Other breweries in Burton had organised trips to the town in previous years, but this was a new destination for the Bass Trips. The date selected was Friday, 17 June 1881. At 4am the first of six Bass trains, supplied by the Midland Railway, left Burton, arriving in Scarborough at 8.40am. The other trains followed at ten-minute intervals, although the last was ten minutes late because of an overheated grease-box. No fewer than 3,500 people made the excursion.

Late the previous day Mr Walters had telegraphed the Meteorological Office for a weather report, which promised that the weather would be dull at first, but clear and fine later. In fact the weather remained dull throughout, but there was no rain. The trippers were provided with a free ticket for dinner at the Scarborough Aquarium at midday. Meals were eaten in batches of three hundred at a sitting, for which the Aquarium caterer supplied 3,750lbs of beef, 6,000 dinner rolls, 24 gallons of pickles, six dozen bottles of Worcester sauce and 1,000 veal and ham pies. In addition to the free meal each man was given one shilling (boys sixpence) and a day's wages. Moreover, on production of the excursion ticket free admission was given to the Aquarium and Spa, where various entertainments were provided, and free rides were available on the South Cliff tramway. The free entertainments were provided at the expense of Bass, Ratcliff & Gretton, and were subject to negotiation prior to the Trip. At the end of the day the first train started the return journey from Scarborough to Burton at 6.10pm and the last arrived home at the relatively early hour of 12.50am.

Reporting the Scarborough visit, the *Burton Weekly News and Advertiser* burst into poetry:

'The name of Bass — omnipotent —
Along the line the coaches sent,
With goodly speed and small delay,
As any man could wish or pray,
Until we reached our journey's end,
With W.Walters, guide and friend,
Who wisely saw the folks he led,
Were entertained and all well fed.'

The Annual Trips Begin

THE original Midland Railway Station in Burton upon Trent had become extremely congested by the late 1870s, handling in addition to passengers and general goods great quantities of beer. Because of this, several of the Bass Trips had departed from the sidings in the timber yard on Mosley Street. However, after 1883 the Burton brewery trips were able to use the facilities of the rebuilt station. This was designed as an island, giving two platforms, by the Midland Railway's architect, Mr Saunders, and constructed by Cox of Leicester. The Station Street level crossing was replaced by a new road bridge constructed under the supervision of Mr Campion, the Midland's engineer. Booking office facilities were provided at bridge level for the Midland, London & North Western, North Staffordshire and Great Northern Railway companies.

Messrs Bass & Co's Biennial excursion ran to London in 1883, carrying 3,500 passengers in six trains. The usual gratuities were allowed and cheap tickets were available for the Fisheries Exhibition (9d) and the Zoological Gardens (6d). About a thousand people went to each. There was also cheap admission to Madame Tussaud's and the Westminster Aquarium.

By this time, the Bass Trips were unusual in being held every other year, perhaps a consequence of their size which was by now far in excess of any other brewery excursion from Burton upon Trent. But all this was to change. Although 1884 was regarded as a bye-year for the Bass Trip, the holding of a special exhibition in Wolverhampton prompted the idea of a visit for the workforce on 30 August, five trains being used for the half-day Trip. The number of passengers is not recorded, but would have been about 2,500-3,000, judging from the size of the other Trips. The first train left at noon, travelling via Tamworth and Water Orton. It was raining as the party arrived in Wolverhampton, but this soon cleared up and the Bass trippers joined the crowds from elsewhere. The Burton Volunteer Band played

and was well received. The *Burton Weekly News and General Advertiser* of 4 September 1884 commented: 'The townspeople appreciated the influx of visitors, for things were suspended from bedroom windows, welcoming Messrs Bass & Co's employees.'

The exhibition in question was the Wolverhampton and Staffordshire Fine Arts and Industrial Exhibition which took place from May to October 1884 in the town's Art Gallery and in two temporary buildings erected nearby, housing respectively Fine Arts, Machinery, along with Archaeological and Geological exhibits.

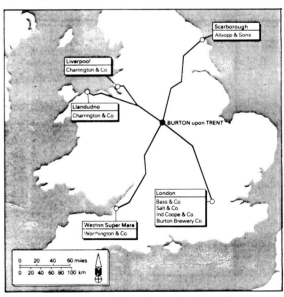

The Burton Brewery Excursions in 1883. The summer months were recognised as the brewery excursion season in Burton upon Trent, when all the major brewing firms gave treats for their employees in the form of organised railway excursions. The position of Burton in relation to the railway network enabled the brewers to offer a wide variety of destinations within easy reach for a day excursion. The map shows the destinations chosen in 1883, when Bass sent six trains to London, also visited by Salt, Ind Coope and the Burton Brewery Company. The continuing growth in size of the Bass Trips meant that they were eventually confined to a choice of four destinations — Blackpool, Liverpool, Scarborough and Great Yarmouth — all resorts which could offer sufficient accommodation and facilities for thousands of people, particularly important if the weather was wet.

In 1883 the new station at Burton upon Trent was ready for use, replacing the original structure of 1839. The booking office facilities were placed on a road bridge which eliminated the Station Street level crossing. A large flight of stairs linked the booking hall to the island platform. The Bass Specials regularly departed from the north side of the station, seen in these views taken from the Bass Trip handbook of 1906.

Blackpool was visited for the first time by the Bass Trip in 1885, a venue which was to prove particularly popular over the following years. The *Blackpool and Fleetwood Gazette* reported that when it became known that Blackpool was the destination, applications came for tickets in such numbers that Mr Walters had to increase the number of trains from six to eight, and could have filled a ninth if the railway company had been able to provide it.

In the view of the *Burton Weekly News and General Advertiser* the next year (1886) should have been a bye-year, but the Bass Trip had now become established as an annual event.

It is interesting to compare the earlier photographs with this view taken in May 1965, before a third rebuilding of the station took place. Very little had changed over eight decades; even the lower quadrant signal with its stylish finial appears to be the same.   A.T.Moss

An unidentified train, but probably a Bass Special, awaits departure from Burton. The top-hatted stationmaster is talking with the footplate crew.

Blackpool was first visited by the Bass Trip in 1885. The Tower did not exist and the South Beach was the haunt of fortune-tellers, who have attracted a queue of customers in this early photograph.

This time the destination was London, to visit the Colonial and Indian Exhibition at South Kensington. Each man was given his rail ticket and underground ticket, plus the usual gratuity of 2s 6d and a day's wages. Higher grades were treated at a better rate. This was the last year that London was visited. The following year, on Friday, 17 June, the Bass Trip went to Liverpool with 4,500 passengers crammed into eight trains. Again the attraction was a large

exhibition being held in a garden setting at Edge Lane to celebrate the Golden Jubilee of Victoria's reign.

The south coast resort of Brighton, where Captain John Anderson was the Bass Agent, was selected for the Trip of 1888, a decision probably influenced by his friendship with Lord Burton. For the first time the number of trains chartered reached double-figures, which gave a little more space for some of the 4,500 passengers. As with all excursions which started early in the morning the intending trippers were wakened by the sound of bugles in the streets of Burton, but this year they were

A rough sea breaking by the Brighton Aquarium, almost engulfing a car on the electric railway opened by Magnus Volk in 1883.   East Sussex County Library.

The Brighton Aquarium and East Cliff in the 1880s. The Bass Trip visited Brighton in 1888, but suffered very wet weather on the day. The Burton Volunteer Band was able to play under cover in the Aquarium and the Pavilion, but because of inadequate shelter the majority of trippers were soaked. The Bass Trips never returned to the south coast.   East Sussex County Library.

earlier than ever, the bugles being heard before 2.30am to ensure that the first train got away with its full complement of passengers at 3.50am. Nine trains had fourteen coaches and the tenth had fifteen; there was a family saloon on each train for the use of the Head of Department and his friends. Midland Railway locomotives took the trains to Rugby, where they were replaced by Webb compounds of the L&NWR, running as far as Kensington, where London, Brighton & South Coast locomotives took over. The short section of line onwards to Clapham Junction could not be negotiated by bogie carriages, so the trains were made up of five-bodied third-class vehicles, which probably lacked some of the comforts of the later type. The overall journey time was about four and three-quarter hours, which was a very creditable performance.

The trippers were met at Brighton by Captain Anderson, who was reported to be 'genial and cheery as ever'. He chaired the Company luncheon at the Royal Pavilion Hotel, while W.H.Bailey (who was appointed London Agent later in the year) was vice-chairman. Bailey was a popular after-dinner speaker and chaired many of the future Trip luncheons. Unfortunately the weather was against the trippers — it poured down all day. Mr Walters later described it as 'a shocking wet day'. His son, E.C. (Joe) Walters, recalled the visit. He was eleven at the time and was one of the fortunate few who escaped the rain by attending the luncheon given by Messrs Bass & Co for their Agents, local dignitaries and representatives of the railway companies with which they did so much business, about a hundred people in all. The Burton Volunteer Band also avoided the rain by playing in the Aquarium and Pavilion instead of the outdoor bandstands, but the other 4,400 trippers were less fortunate. They were forced to wander about in the pouring rain, because there was insufficient cover for them in the resort. They were drenched and their clothes were still wet when they arrived home in Burton, thoroughly disgruntled after a very long day. Brighton was never visited again.

The Brighton experience demonstrated the necessity of selecting resorts within easy reach of the Midlands and which possessed adequate shelter and entertainments for the size of excursion being run by Bass. From now on the choice was limited to the four destinations of Liverpool, Blackpool, Scarborough and (from 1893) Great Yarmouth.

The Later Excursions

THE concentration of the later Bass excursions on the four principal destinations meant that some of the organisational work was eased, as the railway companies became used to the demands made upon them and the resorts themselves were able to respond with a package of entertainments for the visitors. The size of excursions continued to grow. On four occasions no less than seventeen trains were used from Burton upon Trent (three times to Blackpool and once to Liverpool), while in 1896 and 1905 the special train carrying the London Agency party again brought the total Bass trains to seventeen. The greatest number of trippers carried on one day was 11,241 in 1900, the destination being Blackpool.

Over the years the excursion handbooks became more comprehensive, offering information about the route travelled by the trains, the rolling stock provided by the railway companies, full details of the day's entertainment programme and general advice about safe and sober conduct. Although much of the material could be used on subsequent occasions the handbooks were updated annually and gave scope for some interesting anecdotes from Mr Walters. But comments in the handbooks also indicate that behaviour was not always of the required standard and that the patience of Mr Walters was tried on several occasions by trippers deliberately missing the earlier trains home, so leading to overcrowding on the later Specials. This was particularly a

4

Very Important.

IT is IMPERATIVE that all persons should TRAVEL BOTH WAYS by their OWN TRAIN. Changing to other Trains, and particularly staying for LATER TRAINS cannot be allowed, as such irregularities upset the arrangements, and seriously interfere with the comfort of the proper occupants of such Trains. All persons detected breaking this URGENT regulation will be LEFT BEHIND at Burton or Blackpool, as the case may be, and the EXCURSION TICKET WILL BE FORFEITED. By the number on the Ticket I can tell conclusively to what Train the holder belongs. It must be distinctly understood that I will NOT undertake to provide room in other Trains for persons who deliberately disregard this most important instruction.

Serious notice will be taken of any breach of this Urgent Regulation.

Accommodation will be reserved in each Train for the exclusive use of the Heads of Departments and others in charge of the men travelling by that Train.

Caution.

Do not throw anything out of the Windows of the Carriages.—It is hoped that no Person will throw Empty Bottles, &c., out of the Carriage Windows, especially whilst the Trains are in motion, as such a proceeding is highly dangerous to the Platelayers and others employed on the Railway. Empty Bottles, Paper, &c., should be left in the Racks, or under the Seats of the Carriages.

Do not throw away Lighted Matches.—It is a most dangerous practice, and I recently saw a lady's dress completely ruined, to say nothing of the risk to life, by a lighted match being thrown by a smoker under the dress setting the lining on fire. Fortunately the smoke was discovered and the fire extinguished. Be careful, therefore, to put out all lighted matches before throwing them down on the floors of the Carriages, the Platforms, or in the Streets.

Do not throw Orange Peel on the Platforms or Pavements.—It is very dangerous to passers-by, and serious accidents have happened to persons treading on it and then slipping down.

May I specially beg of all persons to be quiet and orderly on the journeys, on the Steamers, at the various Places of Amusement, in the Streets, and generally throughout the day? It should be remembered that we have visited Blackpool on previous occasions; let it, therefore, be again said that Bass & Co's. Employees knew how to behave themselves, and that all returned home perfectly orderly and sober.

Instructions to Blackpool trippers, 1900. Over the years the same appeals were made by William Walters for good behaviour, both on the trains and at the destinations. There was always a temptation, particularly at Blackpool, for passengers on the earlier trains to delay their departure, resulting in overcrowding on the later trains.

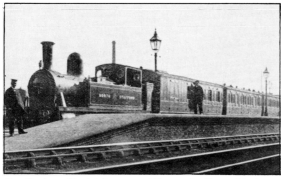

For the benefit of trippers residing at Sudbury, Tutbury, Hatton and Stretton the North Staffordshire Railway provided a special local service (at Bass's expense) with the Tutbury Jenny, which connected at Burton with one of the morning and evening Bass trains.

A view of Vauxhall Station, Great Yarmouth, specially taken for the handbook of 1905. The Bass Specials completely disrupted local services throughout the day, and on the larger excursions needed up to two miles of sidings at the resorts. Other rolling stock would have to be distributed elsewhere for the duration of the visit.

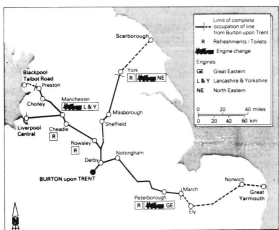

Line occupation by the Bass Trips. The running of the Bass Trips meant a large-scale reorganisation of railway operations around them. With up to 17 trains running at 10-minute headways, full possession of the railway track was necessary for nearly 100 miles from Burton. Spectators would gather along the trackside to watch the progress of the Specials, which could take nearly three hours to pass any one point. The Blackpool trains occupied the track to just beyond Preston, the Scarborough trains as far as York, and the Yarmouth trains to March. Refreshment stops were made en route and engines were changed on all except the Liverpool Trips, which the Midland locomotives worked throughout. Similar arrangements applied to the return journey, although there would have been fewer spectators late at night!

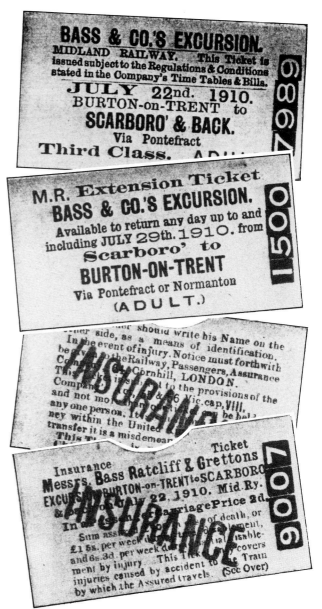

Tickets for the Bass Trip to Scarborough, 22 July 1910. A regular 3rd-Class day-ticket (top) and an Extension ticket allowing travel back to Burton up to a week beyond the original excursion. Mr Walters insisted that all trippers purchased an insurance ticket (below) operated by the Railway Passengers' Assurance Company. He naturally hoped that this would be an unnecessary precaution but felt that 'a bird in the hand is worth two in the bush' so it would be best to be prepared for an emergency.

problem at Blackpool, the most popular of the destinations.

There is no record of the attitude of the Midland Railway Company to the Bass excursions, which is a pity, because of the complexity of arrangements involved. Firstly, the excursions were run on Friday, which was a normal working day for the rest of the railway system. As many as 225 vehicles were required for the larger trips, which would have to be collected from all over the Midland's system. The day before the excursion these would be assembled into trains with each vehicle marshalled into a predetermined order, while as many as seventeen locomotives would be released from other duties and made ready. Up to two miles of sidings were needed to stable the excursions, both in the Burton area and at the resorts. On the day of the Trip the trains were needed in the right order at the right time, already pasted with labels. The loaded trains were then despatched with clockwork precision at ten or fifteen minute intervals. For example, in 1911 fifteen trains were despatched to Blackpool between 3.50am and 6.20am, including No.11 which started from Barton & Walton, calling at Branston, for the benefit of employees at the Estate Farm, Gardens and Stables at Rangemore and Byrkley. In addition there was a special free service on the North Staffordshire line from Tutbury which had to be slotted into the schedules to allow it to connect with train No.13. Trains No.12 and 15 made stops at Willington and Derby to pick up employees and customers. The same arrangements applied in reverse for the homeward journey.

In order to accommodate the Bass Specials the track along the chosen route was usually dedicated to their sole use until the last trains had gone through. In the case of the 1911 Trip to Blackpool, it took two and a half hours for the fifteen Specials to pass any one point. This clearly meant that any other traffic would be delayed or re-routed, both in the morning and evening. But the disruption extended far beyond the Midland system. Engines for the Blackpool trains were provided by the Midland as far as Manchester, where they were exchanged for a similar number from the Lancashire & Yorkshire Company, which then worked the trains over their own route as far as Chorley before joining the L&NWR main line to Preston. Presumably negotiations were necessary between the various companies to allow the smooth passage of the trains over these sections. On the Scarborough excursions similar arrangements would have been made with the Great Northern Railway for access into York Station, where the locomotives were usually exchanged for those of the North Eastern Railway.

Some indication of the disruption caused to regular services in East Anglia by the Bass Trips is given in accounts carried in the *Yarmouth Mercury*. Describing the Trip of 1901, the newspaper noted that the first of the sixteen trains had arrived about fifteen minutes ahead of time. The run from Burton to Yarmouth was scheduled for four hours forty minutes, which some of the earlier trains did in four hours twenty minutes. The trains avoided Norwich by the Wensum curve and then ran direct to Yarmouth both via Acle and Reedham, as traffic requirements dictated.

'So Royally was the excursion planned, that the sole use of the line from Burton to March was handed over to Bass & Co during part of the morning and evening, and at one time there were 13 trains on this section, keeping their regular intervals. No other excursion was run to Yarmouth for the day, and between Norwich and Yarmouth some trains were knocked out of the timetable altogether and the running of others modified, while the Bass Specials were occupying the metals.'

Speaking at the dinner at Yarmouth on 14 July 1905, Mr R.P.Ellis, the Superintendent of the Great Eastern Railway, admitted that a monster excursion to some extent disorganised traffic by monopolising the line in each direction for nearly three hours. He claimed, however, that the public took such an interest in the Trip that they willingly submitted to any temporary inconvenience. But the Bass Specials did not have it all their own way because, on the same day, train No.13 was held up for a few minutes by the local train from Reedham!

On the later visits to Liverpool the Midland locomotives usually worked right through to Central Station over the Cheshire Lines. The Liverpool journey was the shortest of the Bass Trips, even though it used the Midland route through the Peak District. The first train had usually arrived in Liverpool before the last had left Burton. The scale of the operations is best indicated on the map, which shows the maximum amount of track occupied by the Bass Specials as the last train left Burton for each of the four destinations. As can be seen, it was not a case of finding paths for a few extra trains, rather a total re-ordering of railway operations around the Bass Specials.

The ability of William Walters to organise such monster excursions was a reflection of the spending power which the Bass traffic

The turbine steam ship Ben-My-Chree *was one of the ships which carried Bass extension passengers to the Isle of Man in association with the Liverpool Trips.*

department exerted with the railway companies, amounting annually to £250,000 to £300,000. This influence also extended in other directions. In an after-dinner speech at Scarborough in 1894, Mr Walters commented that the railway companies had said that they did not intend to carry any first-class extension passengers in the future. He had replied that under those circumstances Messrs Bass & Co's Trips would not run. The audience laughed and cheered when he added that the railway companies had let it be known that the firsts would be put on as usual *(Burton Evening Gazette* Saturday, 16 June 1894). Clearly the excursion traffic was highly valued by the railways as part of the total brewery traffic generated by the Burton company.

Extension Tickets were available for trippers who wished to spend extra time at the resorts for a proper holiday. They were provided on request at a small extra cost and were valid for the return journey for up to a week after the main excursion. They were to be used on regular connecting services to Burton, but it was the practice, particularly at Blackpool, for special through coaches to be provided on the Monday after the excursion, when it was

reckoned that many extension passengers would return home. If the traffic demanded it, a special express through train to Burton was provided on the following Friday, as at Blackpool in 1907, while in 1911 two extension specials were run.

The Extension Tickets provided remarkable extra value. Passengers from Scarborough were entitled to break their journey at York, while from Great Yarmouth there was a choice of route, either direct over the Midland Railway from Peterborough, or via London, where a stay could be made providing that the return to Burton was made within a week of the excursion. Liverpool passengers could extend their stay at New Brighton, but many chose to take advantage of cheap fares to the Isle of Man. It was, of course, the responsibility of the tripper to pay for board and lodging. The majority of brewery labourers could not afford both the extension tickets and the cost of staying away from home. These facilities were used by the better-paid clerks and officers such as Departmental Heads, which is reflected in the relatively large proportion of first class railway accommodation demanded for the return journeys later in the week.

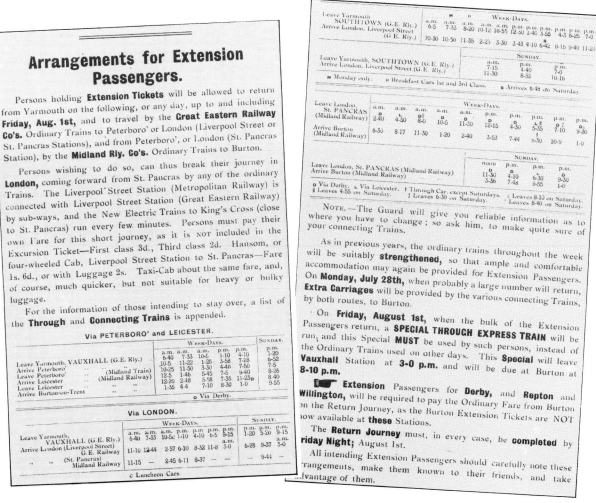

Arrangements for extension passengers from Great Yarmouth, 1913.

Liverpool and New Brighton

What is more enjoyable than the sail of thirty minutes in one of the Wallasey Ferries Steamers?

William Walters, 1904

LIVERPOOL was the destination chosen for the first Bass Trip in 1865 and was visited on nine subsequent occasions, the last being in 1912. It remained a popular venue because of the great variety of attractions which it had to offer. Here was a major city with a wide range of cultural activities, along with the added interest of the bustling port activity. A constant movement of shipping on the Mersey could be viewed from the Pier Head. Across the water lay the growing holiday resort of New Brighton, which in the later years boasted a Tower more than 100 feet taller than the one at Blackpool. The package of attractions on offer to the Bass excursionists varied in detail over the years, but always included free ferry rides to and from New Brighton, free admission to the Tower and

Front cover of the Liverpool Excursion handbook of 1895. The early booklets were inconveniently large, measuring ten by seven and a half inches. By the end of the century they had been reduced to a pocket-sized eight by five inches, but with many pages and copious illustrations.

B.G.Ward.

Liverpool 1908. Train No.8 has just arrived at Central Station and a group of passengers pose somewhat self-consciously for J.S.Simnett, the Burton photographer who for many years accompanied the Bass Trips, providing souvenir postcards and illustrations for the excursion handbooks. Where will they go and what plans have they made for the day? There is not a handbook in sight; presumably the reduction of the publication to pocket-size has proved effective.

Postcard view downstream over the Prince's Docks, Liverpool. In the foreground a ship is receiving attention in a graving dock, some of its lifeboats stacked neatly by the shed in the centre. On the skyline across the mouth of the River Mersey is the outline of New Brighton Tower. Author's collection.

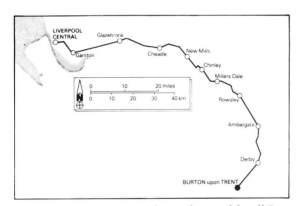

The route from Burton to Liverpool as used by all Bass Trips except the first in 1865. Although not the most direct route, it had the advantage of belonging to the Midland Railway and its associated company, the Cheshire Lines Committee, which perhaps eased the traffic operating problems and certainly avoided disruption of services on the busy section of the LNWR between Crewe and South Lancashire. The Bass Specials to Liverpool were usually worked throughout by Midland Railway locomotives.

Pleasure Gardens, free river trips to view the shipping on the Mersey and free travel on the Liverpool overhead electric railway. This was opened in time for the 1895 trip and gave some spectacular views of the docks along its route.

The sailings of the Isle of Man Steam Packet Company boats to Douglas proved popular over the years. On 14 June 1895 the *Prince of Wales* carried 1,500 Bass trippers on a day's sail to the Isle of Man; Bass employees travelled free, while the cost to their families was a few shillings each. In 1899 the excursion booklet announced that for the first time arrangements had been made with the shipping company for

a free day trip to Douglas for excursionists and for the provision of free return travel for holders of Extension Tickets at considerable expense to the Bass directors. However, from 1902 the Bass excursions were moved into the month of July, which placed them in the main holiday season and meant that the larger vessels were not available for charter for subsequent visits by the Bass trippers, although special reduced fares were on offer. The same kind of arrangements were effected over the years for another popular sea trip, along the coast of North Wales to Llandudno, Beaumaris, Bangor and Menai Bridge. Trips on the Mersey were always well patronised, offering a constantly changing spectacle of shipping and panoramic views of the Liverpool waterfront. In 1891 the trippers were taken to see the work in progess on the Manchester Ship Canal at Eastham and were given special permission to sail along a short length of the new waterway. This visit to Eastham was not repeated in 1899 because, in the words of the handbook, 'there is nothing new to see'.

The Liverpool overhead electric railway aroused the enthusiasm of Mr Walters, who described its construction in detail in the 1895 handbook. The free travel facilities which he negotiated were well used. In 1895 and 1899 there were 15,000 trips made on the railway, while in 1904 there were some 18,000, which represented about two trips for everyone on the excursion that year. The Liverpool Corporation electric tramways provided an alternative source of entertainment in the early years of the new century. In 1908 there were

Construction work on the Liverpool Overhead Railway. This photograph is held in the Bass Museum archives and must have been taken on the express instructions of William Walters, about 1891. In his Trip handbook of 1895, he noted: 'A depot was established at the north end of the railway, where the flooring was constructed and riveted together and to the main girders. The whole span was then raised by jacks, a steam bogey with wheels running upon the two rails nearest the main girder (and thus having a gauge of 16 feet), was run under the span, which, being lowered upon the trolley, was carried by it at such a level as to clear the main girders to the other end of the structure. Arrived at the required point, the span was slung upon a movable gantry, and by it deposited upon the columns prepared to receive it. In this manner span after span was added, as many as ten being placed in a week, representing a length of 500 feet of railway.' This process is captured in the picture. The handbook description must have been hard reading for anyone less than enthusiastic about railways.

The Liverpool Corporation electric tramways offered trippers an alternative source of entertainment in the city. The 1904 booklet recommended four different routes which at modest expense would enable people to travel comfortably in the open air to see the different districts of the city. This picture of car No.234 was published in the 1908 Trip booklet.

four recommended tours of the city, at fares ranging from 4d to 11d. The longest trip ran from Pier Head, through the city centre to Toxteth Park, Dingle, Aigburth and Garston, returning via Prince's Park, Edge Hill, Kensington, Everton, Walton and Aintree to the city. The time needed for this twenty-three and a half mile trip was about two and a half hours for a total fare of 11d.

Shipping on the Mersey was always a major source of fascination and could be viewed from the Pier Head, the overhead railway and the ferries. The excursion handbooks described some of the major ships which might be seen, concentrating particularly upon the trans-Atlantic liners which sailed from the port. It was sometimes possible to gain admission to inspect certain ships on production of the Bass railway ticket. In 1904, the Cunard Company's RMS *Lucania* and RMS *Ivernia* were available for visits in Huskisson Dock, along with the White Star liner RMS *Teutonic*.

Writing in 1912, Mr Walters noted that the excursionists 'will be interested to note that the Cunard S.S. Co. are excellent customers of ours'. He continued, 'During the year their steamers are supplied with over 300,000 pint bottles of "BASS", the larger steamers taking, at the busy season, 10,000 bottles on a round trip.'

The Allan Line and the Canadian Pacific line on the North American run were also good customers for the products of Messrs Bass & Co. Similarly the White Star line, with its liners *Olympic, Megantic* and *Laurentic* to be seen in Liverpool, was also supplied.

The excursion booklet stated: 'Large quantities of "Bottled Bass" are consumed on these floating palaces, and it may be stated that each of the White Star Line steamers sailing from Liverpool to Australia and back to the Old Country — a four months' voyage — is supplied with a little short of 20,000 bottles of "Bass" for the round trip.'

New Brighton

The main attraction for the majority of Liverpool trippers lay across the river at New Brighton. This once sparsely populated area at the tip of the Wirral peninsula had grown rapidly during the nineteenth century, both as a commuter settlement for the city but also as a thriving holiday resort, developments which were enhanced by the establishment of a ferry service and later a direct railway connection to Liverpool.

Writing in 1904 about 'Places of Amusement, Objects of Interest and General Information in the Liverpool area', Mr Walters said: 'New Brighton: I place this place first, as a day's enjoyment is to be had here alone. It is practically a seaside town with the great advantage of being within half-an-hour of Liverpool. What is more enjoyable than the sail of thirty minutes in one of the Wallasey Ferries Steamers?'

The sands of New Brighton were described as unrivalled for their vast stretch, extending to the estuary of the Dee, being firm and safe, an ideal place for children to play. At the end of Victoria Road, next to the Ferry Pier, stood the Promenade Pier (admission free) with its Pavilion offering variety entertainments for a small charge. During the period of the Bass Trips the facilities at New Brighton underwent considerable improvements. The Marine Promenade, extending alongside the river to Seacombe, was continued towards Perch Rock Battery and on to the seaward face of the Wirral, this work being inaugurated in 1907. In the process the notorious 'Ham and Eggs Parade', a row of cafes and other facilities with an unsavoury reputation, was swept away.

The major attraction offered by New Brighton was the Tower and Gardens, upon which work started in June 1896; the grounds were opened at Whitsun 1897 and the Tower in 1900. Free admission was available to the Bass excursionists on presentation of their railway ticket. This gave access to the Tower itself, which offered splendid views across the Mersey and surrounding countryside from a height of 621ft above sea-level. The main building contained a Theatre, Ball Room, Billiard Saloon and souvenir stalls. There was a programme of free entertainments throughout the day. The Tower Gardens in

The train arrangements for the Bass Trip to Liverpool on Friday, 16 June 1899. A study of these shows the complexity and precision of operations. Train No.13 links with the Tutbury Jenny special working, No.14 takes domestic and estate staff from the Bass family homes, while No.16 carries Mr Walters and his entourage.

New Brighton beach. The resort had everything that the trippers needed — sand, sun and fun, and plenty to eat and drink. The sands were described as firm and safe, unrivalled for their vast stretch, from the Mersey to the estuary of the Dee. In 1899 twenty donkeys, marked with red rosettes, were available free for the Bass women and children. The Rock lighthouse, which had guarded the Mersey since 1830, was open for visitors at low tide. Bathing machines were for hire at 6d (2½p) per person or 4d per person if two or more shared the same van. Mr Walters offered words of advice to potential bathers, including recognition of the signs that they had been in the water too long — shivering and blueness of the skin, stiffness in the fingers and chattering of the teeth, giddiness, headache, loss of appetite, and depression of spirits. The necessary course of action would be to dress quickly and obtain a pail of hot water for the feet, to restore the circulation! Liverpool City Libraries.

1904 contained an ornamental lake with Venetian Gondolas, complete with native gondoliers, a restaurant at Rock Point Castle and an Old English Fairground, where the attractions included the Himalaya Railway, the only one of its kind in the north and said to produce 'a most exhilarating effect on the pasengers who travel round it.' There was the Menagerie and Lion House, a water chute down which boats could be ridden into the lake and, for the more energetic customers, a cycle-track open throughout the day. New attractions were introduced to the Gardens and in 1908 these included Sir Hiram Maxim's 'Flying Airships', a Figure-8 Gravity Road and a monster Scenic Railway. The negotiations carried out by Mr Walters included closing the Tower and Gardens early enough to ensure that the excursionists left New Brighton in

sufficient time to catch their trains home from Liverpool.

The Liverpool newspapers reported most of the Bass visits over the years, although no mention can be found of the trips in 1873, 1899 or 1912. The *Liverpool Daily Post* carried a lengthy account of the visit of 1908, describing the 8,500 trippers as representing an 'invasion of Liverpool'. It was noted that arrangements had again been made for free travel on the Overhead Railway, the ferries and fairground amusements at New Brighton Tower. The *Liverpool Daily Post* commented that Bass's had bought up practically all the local rolling and heaving stock for the day!

Two accidents were reported on the 1908 trip, although neither was mentioned in the Burton Press. In the midst of the good-natured jostling and jollification at Central Station on the

New Brighton on a Bank Holiday in 1888. The best way to reach the resort was by ferry from Liverpool and in this view pasengers can be seen on the left pouring from the landing stage. On their right is the Promenade Pier, not very busy even though a return ferry ticket gave free admission to the amusements. Ahead lies Victoria Road, lined with shops, while to the right and overlooking the beach is 'Ham 'n' Eggs Parade', a line of cheap cafes and boarding houses with a notorious reputation for certain other types of entertainment.   Liverpool City Libraries.

homeward journey, one man got a bad knock while crushing into one of the carriages. The second incident occurred at New Brighton. One of the ladies in the party stood on her dress whilst descending the big flight of stairs at the Tower fairground. She fell heavily, breaking an arm and suffering abrasions and shock. She was taken to Central Station on a stretcher and sent home on the first available train.

Much has changed at New Brighton since the days of the Bass Trips. The Tower was dismantled between May 1919 and June 1920, after years of neglect had rendered it unsafe. The Tower buildings and grounds still provided a wide range of entertainments until the 1960s, but in 1969 the main building was badly damaged by fire and later demolished. The funfair was abandoned and eventually most of the grounds were developed for housing. The ferry landing stage and amusement pier were closed and removed in the 1970s, leaving only a small remnant of the once-extensive attractions which brought thousands of holiday-makers every year. In the 1990s, New Brighton is largely ignored by the tourist and the main thoroughfare, Victoria Road, for many years a dismal picture of derelict shops, is being developed as a local shopping centre. A major factor in the decline of the resort has been the disappearance of the beach, because of coastal erosion in recent years, which has left only an expanse of polluted mud and rock where once the Bass trippers enjoyed a relaxing day on the sands, with the occasional dip in the sea from a bathing machine.

New Brighton Tower, which became the resort's greatest tourist attraction, viewed from the Rock lighthouse. The fantasy outline of the Tower contrasts sharply with the squat block of Fort Perch Rock to the left. The Tower reached a height of 621ft, more than 100ft taller than the rival Tower at Blackpool. Work started on the building in 1896, the grounds were opened in the following year and the Tower itself by 1900. On Bass Trip days the Tower and gardens were open for the exclusive use of the visitors from Burton, with free admission to all facilities. Sadly, neglect of maintenance during the First World War left the structure in a dangerous condition. This photograph was taken on an early summer's afternoon in 1919; within a year the iron Tower had disappeared, but the main building at the base survived until the 1960s. Liverpool City Libraries.

25

Special Programme of Entertainments.

The Grounds will be opened on the arrival of the first Steamer from the Landing Stage.

9-0. On Platform facing Sea.

The **MILITARY BAND** will play

1.	MARCH	...	"Under the double Eagle" ...	WAGNER
2.	OVERTURE	...	"Light Cavalry" ...	... SUPPE
3.	VALSE	...	... "Tris Iolie" ...	WALDTEUFEL
4.	SELECTION		"Reminiscences of Ireland"	——
5.	POLKA	...	"Fun of the Fair" ...	AIGRETTE
6.	GAVOTTE	...	... "Stephanie" ...	CZIBULKA
7.	INDEX	...	... "Mors et Vita" ...	GOUNOD
8.	BALLET	...	"William Tell" ...	... ROSSINI

The Concert will end at 11-0, when the **Hungarian Band** will play as below.

10-0. Exhibition of the Famous Polverini Cinematograph, when the following Animated Pictures will be shown.

1. A Storm at the Breakwater.
2. Grenadier Guards entering the Tower of London.
3. The Seaforth Highlanders leaving Alexandria for Khartoum.
4. The Grand National, 1898. Run in a Snow-storm.
5. A Pillow Fight.
6. The Fire Brigade.
7. A Mail Train travelling at 70 miles an hour.
8. H.M. the Queen leaving Netley Station on her return from Netley Hospital, on the occasion of her visit to Piper Findlater (the hero of Dargai) who was presented with the Victoria Cross.

This Exhibition will be repeated at 11-0, 12-0, 1-0, 2-0, 3-0, 4-0 and 5-0 o'clock.

11-0. The HUNGARIAN BAND will perform the following selection on Platform facing the sea.

1.	MARCH	"Honest Toil"		RIMMER
2.	OVERTURE ...	"Isolda"	...	VERNER
3.	VALSE	"Brotherhood" ...	...	POGSON
4.	SELECTION ...	"Gems of Cambria"	...	ROUND
5.	GLEE	"Strike the Lyre"	...	COOKE
6.	LANCERS	"A Giddy Night"	...	WILLIAMS
7.	TROMBONE SOLO	"The Grand"	...	JUBB
8.	POLKA	"Star of Denmark"	..	... GIFFARD

The Concert will conclude at 1-0, when the Military Band will perform on the dancing platform. See Programme below.

12-0 Noon. Cinematograph Exhibition takes place as per programme.

The **Himalaya Electric Railway** and famous **Water Chute** run all day. Visitors will be admitted on production of Ticket.

1-0. The Military Band will perform on the Dancing Platform as follows :—

1.	MARCH	...	"Liberty Bell"	
2.	OVERTURE ...	"William Tell"	...	... SOUSA
3.	VALSE	... "Beautiful May"	...	... ROSSINI
4.	SELECTION	"Reminiscences of Scotland"		STRAUSS
5.	POLKA MAZURKA	"Alpine Rose"		——
6.	LANCERS ...	"The Mikado"	...	STRAUSS
7.	VALSE	... "Hofball Tanze" ...	...	SULLIVAN
8.	THREE DANCES FROM HENRY VIII		...	FETRAS
			...	GERMAN

The Concert will conclude at 3-0, when the celebrated "Tower String Orchestra" will play Dance Music in the Grand Ball Room.

1-0. Professor Ted Heaton, Fair Ground, Wonderful Dive.

2-0. Variety Performance in the **Grand Theatre** when the following Programme will be presented. Admission on production of Ticket. (First Class Passengers only will be admitted to the Front Reserved Seats).

1.   **MISS EMMIE AMES**
The Popular Burlesque Actress, Vocalist and Dancer.
2.   **MADDEN & WOOD**
The Clever Comedy Team from America in an original Burlesque Sketch.
3.   **DAVID DAVIS**
The World's Siffleur introducing his well-known imitation of Singing Birds.
4.   **FRANCIS GERARD**
(From the Nouveau Cirque, Paris). The most daring and skilful Athlete and Equilibrist known.
5.   **DREW & ALDERS**
The Renowned Pantomimic Speciality. These artistes stand unrivalled as Comic Acrobats, and give a unique and finished performance.
6.   **ORVEN & WILLIAMS**
Descriptive Duettists.
7.   **THE FOUR AMERICAN BELLES**
Speciality Vocalists.
8.   **CHARLES CRASTON**
Comedian.
9.   **PROF. TED HEATON**
Swimming Act.
10.   **GIBSUN**
A Sensational Speciality from the Antipodes. The Australian Bushman in his unique performance of juggling, rifle swinging, and play with keen edged axes.

3-0. Cinematograph Exhibition. See programme.

3-0. The Celebrated **Tower String Orchestra** will perform the following music in the Grand Ball Room :—

1.	VALSE	...	...	...	...	...	...	STRAUSS
2.	ARIA	...	...	...	...	...	...	BACH
3.	MINUET	...	...	...	...	...	...	BOCHESINI
4.	PETITE WALTZ ...		...	...	...	...	TSCHAIKOWSKY
5.	SERENADE...	...	...	...	...	...	...	ELGAR
6.	VALSE	...	...	...	...	...	...	WALDTEUFEL
7.	TWO MELODIES, a.b.		...	...	...	...	...	GRIEG
8.	WALSER ...	...	...	...	...	...	...	BRAHMS

The concert concludes at 5-0, when the Military Band will play on the dancing platform.

Dancing in the Ball Room will commence at 5-0, immediately after the afternoon concert.

4-0. Cinematograph Exhibition as per programme. **The Athletic Grounds** will be open to all visitors presenting their tickets at the gates.

5-0. Last exhibition of the **Cinematograph**, as per programme.

5-0. Professor Ted Heaton, Fair Ground, Wonderful Dive.

Dancing in the Grand Ball Room until 6-30 p.m. whilst the **Military Band** will at **5-0** perform the following Selections on the Dancing platform :—

1.	GRAND MARCH	"Tannhauser"	...	WAGNER
2.	VALSE	... "Ballscenen"	...	CZIBULKA
3.	LANCERS ...	"The Savoy"	...	SULLIVAN
4.	SCHOTTISCHE	"Popcorn"	...	... LATH
5.	SELECTION	"Reminiscences of England"	...	...
6.	HUSSARENWITT	...	...	...	SPINDLEY
7.	VALSE	"Moonlight on the Rhine"	VOLLSTEDT
8.	GALOP	... "Princesse Marie" ...	D'ALBERT

This concert will conclude about 6-30.

Special entertainments were laid on at the New Brighton Tower, free to the Bass trippers. This is the programme for the visit of 1895.

Blackpool

Blackpool! The Tower! So predominant and distinctive a feature of Blackpool is the Tower that one is hardly reckoned without the other. Standing stately and stupendous at the very centre of the seafront, the most compelling landmark for many miles around, the Tower may be looked for as the first sign at the end of our long journey. Soon after leaving Preston, if the weather is fine, we may expect to locate this monument of engineering skill, and, as its summit is brilliantly illuminated after dusk, the Tower will be the last to "beam" us Blackpool's au revoir.

Bass Excursion Handbook 1911

THE Bass Trip went to Blackpool on eight occasions, the first in 1885 and the last in 1911. As with New Brighton, experienced trippers saw the resort flourish during this period. The Tower, 480ft high to the observation deck and 519ft to the top of the flag-pole, was opened in 1894, having consumed six and a half million bricks, 2,493 tons of steel and 93 tons of cast iron in the construction. Two years later a huge wheel was opened in the nearby grounds of the Winter Gardens. Three piers, a Pleasure Beach, various theatres and music halls helped to make Blackpool the biggest and brashest resort of the

Blackpool, famous for fresh air and fun, was always the most popular of the Bass Trips. The Tower was opened in 1894 and was free to Bass trippers on production of the excursion ticket. A combination of high tide and strong westerly winds could create spectacular seas, as this postcard shows. In addition to the Tower, Blackpool also boasted a huge revolving wheel, 250ft high, opened in 1896. A total of 900 people could enjoy the panoramic views during a sixteen-minute ride, but it was never a great success and was dismantled in 1928.　　　Author's collection.

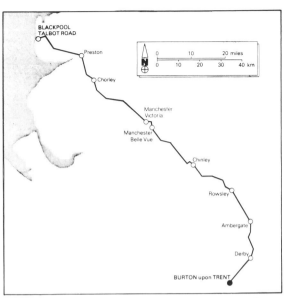

The Bass journeys from Burton to Blackpool passed over the metals of the Midland, Great Central, Lancashire & Yorkshire and London & North Western Companies. Locomotives were exchanged at Philips Park sidings, Miles Platting, where L & Y locomotives took over from the Midland engines. A five-minute stop was allowed for refreshments in both directions, giving a total journey time of three and a half hours. On Friday, 15 June 1900, some 11,000 trippers were carried to Blackpool by 17 Bass Special trains, the largest number of Bass passengers carried in a single day.

age, while the broad promenade and excellent sandy beach made this the most popular venue for the Bass trippers. It was at Blackpool that Mr Walters experienced the most difficulty in trying to persuade trippers to join the earlier trains home, the temptation to stay for a few more hours proving irresistible to many.

Blackpool seemed to offer the best value for the trippers in terms of free admissions and reductions negotiated by Mr Walters and his assistants, Messrs Lyle and Eley. The programme for Friday, 19 July 1907 offered free admission to the Tower and its various attractions, including the Menagerie, Ballroom and Roof Gardens. The Circus performance was too expensive for the Bass trippers to be given free seats, but a reduced scale of charges was available on production of the railway ticket. Free entertainments were available in the Winter Gardens, the Palace Theatre and on the Piers, from where a busy schedule of steamers provided trips out to sea. In what appeared to be a gruelling schedule lasting from 8am to the early evening, a break of fifteen minutes for lunch was built into the programme! In practice the trippers were expected to choose their activities from the menu which was offered to them.

For many people a visit to the seaside would be incomplete without a dip in the sea. Accordingly Mr Walters arranged for bathing machines to be available at each of the resorts visited, while cautioning the readers of his handbook about the possible dangers involved.

It is hardly daylight when the first Bass train arrives at the excursion platforms next to Talbot Road station in Blackpool. However, the weather is brighter by the time that train No.5 arrives and the sun is out for Nos.10 and 12. The views give tantalising glimpses of the Lancashire & Yorkshire locomotives. Train No.1 is possibly hauled by locomotive No.83. The others cannot be identified.

This well-known picture sums up the scale and complexity of the railway operations involved in the Bass Trips. The date is Friday, 12 June 1896. Bass Specials Nos.1 to 8 are lined up from right to left at the excursion platforms at Talbot Road, Blackpool, ready for the return journey to Burton. On the far right is Train No.17 which carried members of the Bass London Agency to join the 10,000 trippers at the seaside. The trains will leave at ten-minute intervals and their places will be taken by the other eight trains, requiring some smart work from the carriage sidings. The regular station platforms are on the left. The Tower looms dimly in the background and to the left is Blackpool Parish Church. National Railway Museum, York.

For example, at Blackpool in 1907 he advised his patrons that bathing machines would be available for Ladies and Gentlemen at various points on the North Shore, Central Beach and South Shore. These were not free but were charged at 1s per person, or 6d each if more than one person used the machine at a time.

The handbook stated: 'From the time of arrival of No.1. Special it will be suitable for bathing. But let me repeat my warning of previous years — Not to bathe for less than two hours after taking a hearty meal; and after bathing do not stand about, but take a sharp walk. This is especially necessary after a warm salt-water bath, when the pores of the skin are open, and a chill may be easily taken.'

The Blackpool and Fleetwood Tramroad was opened on 13 July 1898 and special travel facilities were arranged with the proprietors for the benefit of the Bass Excursionists. In Blackpool the trams started in Dickson Road, close to the Talbot Road Station, but the Bass people were advised to join the cars at the Gynn Inn, from where express cars ran through to Fleetwood. A concessionary return fare of 6d (the normal single fare) was available on presentation of the railway ticket at the Gynn booking office, valid on the day of the excursion only. At Fleetwood it was possible to take the

short ferry ride across the River Wyre to Knott End, for a drive into the country to the village of Pilling. In 1903 this service was provided by horse-drawn brakes, but — a sign of the times — by 1907 there was a motor coach service for Pilling at 6d each way. An alternative attraction at Fleetwood was a cruise on the River Wyre in a new service operated by motor launches.

It is from Blackpool that the only evidence of any real local dissatisfaction with the Bass Trips is found. The problem lay in the use of the railway excursion tickets — the "Open Sesame" for the free attractions and entertainments on offer. Clearly some trippers, who had failed to read their handbooks carefully, took an expansive view of the use of the little ticket.

In a rather sour article the *Blackpool and Fleetwood Gazette* of Tuesday, 16 June 1896 reported: 'The business people do not look back to Friday with any great degree of pleasure. They say the men from the Brewery brought no money with them and were too ready to produce the omniscient tickets provided by Mr Walters.

'Our Burton friends thought this entitled them to participate in every imaginable thing. They mounted the electric trams and rode

Bass paddlers, 1903.

Patronising the ice-cream van on Blackpool's central beach, 1903.

serenely until asked for the fare — then out came the ticket. They joined the merry laughter at the quips and cracks of the niggers and when the mock Ethiopian came round for the usual thanks-offering — out came the tickets. Punch and Judy entertained them, and to the surprise of our venerable friends when he sent the hat round — out came the tickets. Four men, we are told, hailed a landau, comfortably seated themselves, and told John to take them for a drive. "Whereto?" he said, "Anywhere," they said. "I'll take you to St Annes for ten bob," proposed the Cabby. "What!" said the Burtonians, "Ten Bob; why, we are Bass's from Burton —" and out came the tickets. Goodness only knows what the Brewers thought they could obtain with this.'

The same edition of the Blackpool newspaper carried a report of proceedings in the local Magistrates Courts on the day of the

"Let us live to-day, and enjoy all its benefits. Let us live to-day, and be true to all its responsibilities. Let us live to-day, and use all the strength that we have to make this day the most complete day of our lives."

Synopsis of the Amusements, &c.

This Table will show at a glance what is going on throughout the day.

FROM A.M.	TO P.M.		See Pages.
7-30	...	The First Train arrives at No. 9 Excursion Platform—see Trains Sheet	8 to 9
8-0	7-0	The Tower. Lifts, Aquarium, Menagerie, Monkey House and Aviary, Ball Room, Roof Gardens, &c.	51-56
8-0	7-0	The Palace. Theatre of Varieties, Monkey Houses, Ball Room, Pictures, Panopticum, &c.	57-59
8-0	7-0	The Winter Gardens. Pavilion, Empress Ball Room, Indian Lounge, Fernery, &c.	60-64
8-0	7-0	The North Pier. Steamers, Orchestras and Variety Entertainments	65-67
8-0	7-0	The Central Pier. Steamer, Bands for Dancing...	67-68
8-0	7-0	The Victoria Pier. Berlin Meister Orchestra and Variety Entertainments	69-70
8-0	7-0	Arbury's (South Beach Baths). Large Tepid Swimming Bath. Open (Gentlemen only) Free. Private Baths, Ladies or Gentlemen, 1s. each ...	81-82
10-0	12-0	The North Pier. Royal Roumanian Band in the Arcade ...	65-67
10-0	12-30	The Central Pier. Bands for Dancing... ...	67-68
10-30	1-0	The North Pier. Open-Air Promenade Concert	65-67
10-30	...	The Last Train arrives at No. 2 Excursion Platform— see Trains Sheet	8 to 9
11-0	1-0	The Victoria Pier. Variety Entertainment in the Pavilion	69-70

INTERVAL FOR DINNER.

P.M.			
1-15	...	Steamers "Greyhound" and "Belle" leave the North Pier Jetty for Trips to Sea	71-73
1-45	...	Steamer "Bickerstaffe" leaves the Central Pier Jetty for Trip to Sea	71-73
2-0	4-0	The Winter Gardens. Grand Ballet "By the Zuyder Zee" and Variety Entertainment in the Victoria Pavilion	60-64
2-30	...	Steamers "Greyhound" and "Belle" leave the North Pier Jetty for Trips to Sea	71-73
2-30	4-30	The Tower. Concert and Variety Entertainment in the Ball Room, and Variety Entertainment in the Roof Gardens...	51-56
2-30	...	The Palace. Variety Entertainment in the Theatre— Dancing in the Ball Room	57-59
2-30	4-30	The Winter Gardens. Orchestra in the Empress Ball Room for Dancing...	60-64
2-30	4-30	The North Pier. Royal Roumanian Band in the Arcade...	65-67
3-0	...	Steamer "Bickerstaffe" leaves the Central Pier Jetty for Trip to Sea	71-73
3-0	4-30	The North Pier. Variety Entertainment in the Indian Pavilion	65-67
3-0	5-0	The Central Pier. Bands for Dancing	67-68
3-0	5-0	The Victoria Pier. Variety Entertainment in the Pavilion	69-70
4-0	...	Steamers "Greyhound" and "Belle" leave the North Pier Jetty for Trips to Sea	71-73
4-15	...	Steamer "Bickerstaffe" leaves the Central Pier Jetty for Trip to Sea ...	71-73
5-15	...	Steamers "Greyhound" and "Belle" leave the North Pier Jetty for Last Sea Trips	71-73
5-28	...	High Water. Height of Tide 21 feet 6 inches ...	89
5-30	...	Steamer "Bickerstaffe" leaves the Central Pier Jetty for Last Sea Trip	71-73
*7-0	...	The Tower. Variety Entertainment in the Roof Gardens, and Dancing in the Ball Room	51-56
*7-0	...	The Palace. Variety Entertainment in the Theatre— Dancing in the Ball Room	57-59
*7-0	...	The Winter Gardens. Grand Ballet "By the Zuyder Zee" and Variety Entertainment in the Victoria Pavilion, and Dancing in the Empress Ball Room	60-64
*7-0	...	The North Pier. Variety Entertainment in the Indian Pavilion, and Royal Roumanian Band in the Arcade ...	65-67
*7-0	...	The Central Pier. Bands for Dancing ...	67-68
*7-0	...	The Victoria Pier. Vocal and Instrumental Concert in the Pavilion	69-70
8-0	...	No. 1 Train leaves No. 9 Excursion Platform—see Trains Sheet	8 to 9
10-40	...	The Last Train leaves No. 2 Excursion Platform—see Trains Sheet	8 to 9

* Only Persons presenting EXTENSION TICKETS will be admitted to these Entertainments.

ALL the above will be absolutely FREE on production of the Railway Ticket.

All Day.	For Left Luggage Room at Excursion Platforms ...	... 84-85
,,	Hotels, Restaurants, Dining Rooms, &c. ...	... 86-88
,,	Lavatory Accommodation ...	... 85
,,	Gigantic Wheel—Half-price—Adults, 3d.; Children, 1d.	... 80
,,	Fleetwood Trams—Half-price, 6d. Return Fare ...	... 74-75
,,	St. Annes and Lytham Trams—Return, Special Fares: St. Annes, 6d. each; Fairhaven and Lytham, 9d. each	... 77-79
,,	Borough Electric Tramway Service ...	76
,,	Cabs, Carriages, Waggonettes, &c.	83-84
,,	Free Library and Reading Room	... 92
7-30	The Opera House	64
7-30	The Grand Theatre	90

2-15 and 7-15 Grand Performance Tower Circus. Prices of Admission— 6d., 1/-, 1/6, and 2/6. Early Doors 1-0 and 6-0 o'clock. 6d. extra to all parts 56

The programme of entertainments throughout the day, Blackpool 1907.

The standards of artistic production of the Trip handbook were greatly improved in later years. The rather dull front cover of the 1903 Blackpool Trip handbook was an exception, the result of a last-minute decision to transfer the visit from Liverpool.

Trip. Before the Bench was William Blake of Burton, who was charged with being drunk and disorderly in Cocker Street at lunch-time. The Bench took into consideration that he was the only one of 10,000 trippers who had come before them. They discharged him, so that he could get home. This seems to have been an extraordinary decision, because in the same sitting a local man, John Lennon, received a fine of 2s 6d with costs, or six days in default, for the same offence!

The Route Map at the back of this Sheet will enable you to follow the Journey throughout.

ALL THE TRAINS will Start from Burton Railway Station (St. Paul's side Platform), and, on returning, from the EXCURSION PLATFORMS (Queen Street), adjoining the Talbot Road Station, BLACKPOOL. For Views see pages 4 and 11, and also at the back of this Sheet.

NOTE.—HAVE YOUR TICKETS READY.—All persons will be required to show their Railway Ticket at the Doors at the Main Entrance, and at the Barriers at the top of the steps, at Burton Station, and none but Excursionists travelling by these Trains will be allowed upon the Platforms. The tickets will also be examined at the Platform Barriers at Blackpool before leaving for Burton, and must be given up at the Barriers at Burton Station AT NIGHT. Persons using the Barton and Walton and Branstone Train, and the Tutbury Special, will, of course, show their Tickets in the morning, and give them up at night when alighting at their own Station. See page 9.

The Foremen and Men employed in the Various Departments, with their Wives and all others for whom they have obtained Tickets, must travel by their OWN Train—both going and returning—as under :—

No. of Train.	DEPARTMENT, &c.	OUTWARD JOURNEY		No. of Platform at which you arrive and from which you depart.	RETURN JOURNEY	
		Depart Burton	Arrive Blackpool.		Depart Blackpool	Arrive Burton
		A.M.	A.M.		P.M.	P.M.
1	Mr. Hodgkinson—Stables and Mr. Ollis Coppersmiths, Platelayers, Tailors, Cloggers, and Wireworkers ..	4.0	7.30	9	8.0	11.30
2	Mr. R. W. Clubb—Repairing Cooperage ..	4.10	7.40	8	8.10	11.45
3	Mr. R. W. Clubb—Steam Cooperage, Mr. Elson Mr. Ollis—Plumbers	4.20	7.50	7	8.20	11.50
4	Mr. J. Clubb—Middle Yard and Shobnall ..	4.30	8.5	6	8.30	MIDNIGHT. 12.0
5	Mr. J. Clubb—except Middle Yard and Shobnall Mr. Ollis—Fitters	4.40	8.10	5	8.40	A.M. 12.10
6	Old Brewery—Mr. Ollis—Shobnall and Shobnall Old Brewery	4.50	8.20	4	8.50	12.20
7	New Brewery and Gas and Electric Works ..	5.0	8.30	3	9.0	12.30
8	Middle Brewery Mr. Ollis—Bricklayers and Painters	5.15	8.45	2	9.10	12.40
9	Mr. Williamson—Railway Department ..	5.25	9.5	1	9.20	12.50
10	Grain Department	5.35	9.15	9	9.30	1.5
11	Mr. Dearle Mr. Ollis—Office and Joiners	5.45	9.25	8	9.40	1.15
12	The Customers This Train will take up and set down Customers at WILLINGTON and at DERBY.	5.55	9.35	7	9.50	1.25
13	The Estate, Farm, Gardens and Stables at Rangemore and Byrkley This Train ONLY will take up and set down at BARTON and WALTON and BRANSTONE.	6.5	9.45	6	9.55	1.35
14	Local Special from Tutbury.	6.15	9.55	5	10.10	1.40
15	Mr. Ollis—Blacksmiths, Excavators, and Wheelwrights This Train will take up and set down Passengers at Willington, and at Derby. Derby Passengers (except Customers) must travel by this Train—both ways.	6.25	10.5	4	10.20	1.50
16	Clerks ..	6.35	10.20	3	10.25	2.0
17	Mr. Walters and Friends ..	6.45	10.30	2	10.40	2.25

Placards will be found affixed to each Train, both at Burton and Blackpool, plainly indicating the number of the Train. There will also be Boards—with the number of each Train—placed on the Indicator at the bottom of the steps leading to the Platform (to the Right hand) at Burton. Prominent Notices will also be found over each of the Excursion Platforms at Blackpool. For Views see over, and pages 4 and 11.

SPECIAL NOTE.—Third Class Passengers must travel—10 in each Compartment—5 on each side—the same as ordinary passengers—and this must be strictly carried out in all the Trains to accommodate the Passengers.

VERY URGENT.—It is imperative that all persons should Travel both Ways by their Own Train, and most urgently does this apply to the Earlier Trains on the Return Journey. The Lancashire and Yorkshire Railway Company are most particular about you travelling by your own Train, and seeing Your Ticket, so be fully prepared at Blackpool at night.

☞ Remember to bring ALL your Railway Tickets, and have them ready at Burton and Blackpool Stations.

For Views of the Excursion Platforms at Talbot Road Station, Blackpool, our Special Cloak Room, Lavatories and Way Out, see back of this Sheet, and pages 4 and 11; and for the direct way from Talbot Road Ordinary Station to these Excursion Platforms—see page 11. For Special Tramway arrangements at Burton, and from and to Gresley and Ashby—see pages 13 and 14, and Special Note at side of this Sheet.

SPECIAL NOTES

TUTBURY.—As the last Train in now timed to arrive at Burton at 2·25 a.m., it is hoped that the Tutbury Local Special will be run as under, instead of as stated on page 9, viz.:—

Leave Burton	..	..	2.30 a.m. (Saturday).
Arrive Stretton and Clay Mills	..	..	2.35
Rolleston	..	..	2.40
Tutbury	..	..	2.50

GRESLEY.—A Car will also leave Gresley Station at 4·25 (the "Rising Sun"), Swadlincote, &c., and return from Burton Station about 2·30 a.m. (Saturday). Fares, each way, from Gresley Station, 10d.; "Rising Sun," 8d.; and from other places as stated on page 14.

ASHBY.—The Return Car to Ashby will probably be able to leave at 2·30 a.m. (Saturday) instead of at 2·45 as stated on page 14.

Bass Trip to Blackpool, Friday, 19 July 1907. Train arrangements for the day.

Great Yarmouth

Passing out of Vauxhall Station I candidly admit the prospect is not inviting.

William Walters, 1893

THE old town of Great Yarmouth stands on the spit of land which diverts the mouth of the River Yare some two miles southwards from its original entry into the North Sea. The river provided an excellent sheltered harbour, which supported an important herring fishing industry during the nineteenth century. On the seaward side of the town are five miles of sandy beach, the principal asset which the town was able to exploit during the latter part of the century.

The introduction of Bank Holidays in 1871 brought large numbers of trippers from the Midlands and London, stimulating the town's development into a popular holiday resort. By the time of the first Bass visit in 1893, most of the attractions regarded as essential for the holiday industry were available. Two Piers, the Wellington and Britannia, offered entertainment, fishing and sea trips, while the latest funfair rides were in evidence. In addition the old town, with its ancient walls and old buildings lining the narrow streets running off the market place, was an attraction to many people, while the harbour was a scene of continually changing activity which could capture the attention of many visitors.

The journey from Burton to Great Yarmouth was the longest undertaken by the Bass Trips, being 182 miles of which one hundred was on Great Eastern track from Peterborough to the coast. The average journey time was about four

Bass Special Train No.12 arrives at Great Yarmouth at 10.30am on Friday, 23 July 1909. They had left Burton at 5.40am, the journey talking 4 hours 50 minutes with a short break at Peterborough. The majority of passengers were workers and their families from Bass's Middle Brewery, while others had joined the train off the Tutbury Jenny.

The beach at Great Yarmouth, looking south. Mr Walters enthused: 'What a splendid Sea front and Promenade it is! the finest in England I think, so broad, straight and imposing, with lovely sands, and the sea always with you! No need for a carriage and pair to go out to find the water, as at all tides it remains close in shore, in fact one can lie down all day by its side and enjoy the splashing of the waves and inhale the Ozone of the North Sea.'

Trips to sea, either in small sailing yawls or by steamer, were a regular and popular feature of the Bass Trips, although for many people the sands were sufficient attraction on a fine day. The Yarmouth Independent *of 19 June 1897 noted that the Trip that year had been blessed by ideal weather — continuous sunshine, with exhilarating breezes — and that 'All day long the big, burly brewer and his buxom wife were joining in the digging operations of the young.'*

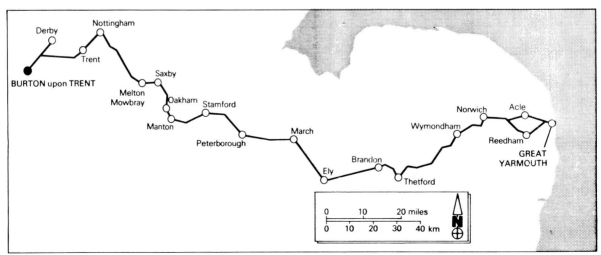

The Bass route to Great Yarmouth. This was the longest journey for the Bass Specials, covering 182 miles from Burton to Great Yarmouth and taking nearly five hours. Engines were changed at Peterborough, where ten minutes were allowed for toilets and refreshments. Temporary counters were set up on the station platform, where tea or coffee (with a slice of bread and butter) could be had for 2d per cup, plain bun 1d, Bath bun 2d, pork pie 4d, not forgetting ale and mineral waters at modest prices.

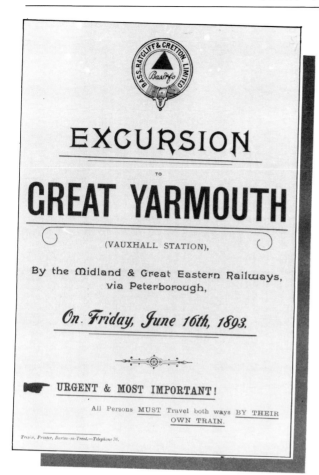

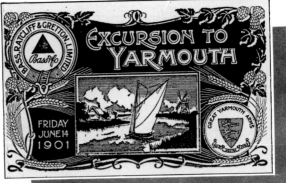

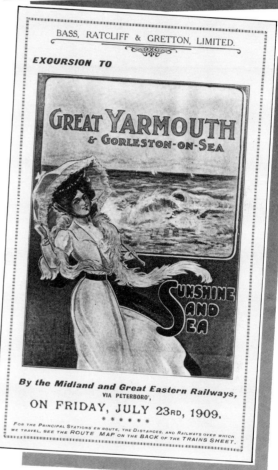

The first Bass trip to Great Yarmouth was also marked by the issuing of the first proper handbook, a fifteen-page publication crammed with information, but without illustrations. Each person was also issued with a copy of The Popular Guide to Great Yarmouth, *profusely illustrated and also a specially prepared town plan.*

and three-quarter hours. In 1893 there were fifteen Bass Specials from Burton, carrying about 8,000 trippers. These were joined by members of the Bass London Agency who for the first time had their own special train. Each excursionist was provided with a copy of a Guide Book to the town, along with the excursion handbook, in which much of the information was summarised at length by Mr Walters.

In his introduction to the town, Mr Walters stated: 'By the kindness of the Directors we are enabled, this year, to open up new ground, the only place on the East Coast previously visited being Scarborough in 1881 and 1890. Let me first of all dispose of two fallacies, pretty generally believed, one is that Yarmouth is only a fishing village, the other is that, although the Midland may run us well to Peterboro', the Great Eastern is a wretched line to travel by. As to the first, Yarmouth (with Gorleston) has a resident population of 50,000 — larger than Burton — and as to the latter, the Great Eastern is the MOST PUNCTUAL line in the kingdom, their express trains travelling quite as quickly as those of the other great Companies!'

The route from Burton took the Castle Donington line to Trent and then to Nottingham, Melton Mowbray, Stamford and Peterborough, where the engines were changed. There was a ten-minute break here, in which time all passengers were able to use the temporary toilet accommodation and obtain refreshments from the counters set up on the platform. It will be remembered that the third-class carriages did not have toilet facilities, hence the importance of the stop! From Peterborough the trains were taken by way of March, Ely and Norwich to Great Yarmouth.

When describing the route for the handbook of 1909, Mr Walters recounted the following story: 'It is related that once upon a time, when trains were slower than they are now, a weary traveller, not catching the name of the station distinctly, put his head out of the window and

Great Yarmouth was famous for its fishing industry, particularly of North Sea herring, which attracted large Scottish fleets at the end of the summer. Two drifters are being towed out to sea by a steam paddle tug.
Author's collection.

shouted, "Porter, where are we?" "March, Sir," replied the porter. "Humph," returned the weary one, "It was February when we started."

Perhaps it was the same sense of humour that led Mr Walters to include in the same handbook a photograph of a new electric train introduced by the Midland Railway on the Lancaster, Morecambe and Heysham Harbour service. He thought that the trippers would be glad to have a picture of the new three car train, which was the first single-phase electric train in the country. However, he was also compelled to add to his usual warnings about the dangers involved in throwing bottles and other objects from the trains a complaint about an incident on the way home from Liverpool the previous year. A small lemonade bottle was thrown from No.14 train and went through the window of St Michael's signal box. Fortunately the signalman was standing at the other end of the box and so escaped injury. (It has been suggested that the lack of toilets on the trains might account for the numbers of bottles flung from the windows.)

Various entertainments were available for the Bass trippers in Yarmouth, including steamer trips, originally from the South Quay and Hall Quay, but following the rebuilding of Britannia Pier the sea trips in 1905 were able to set out directly from there, with a considerable saving in time. In the same year a new attraction was open free to the trippers; this was the Revolving Tower, a passenger compartment which slowly corkscrewed up a tower to an observation platform 150ft high, the machine being equipped with suitable safety brakes. Another popular feature was the switchback railway, as was the Hotchkiss bicycle railway which operated on a circular track.

The handbook stated: 'All who wish can obtain the novelty of a bicycle ride with absolute safety, and those who have not yet ventured on the ordinary safety bicycle should not fail to visit this railway. The bicycles run on wheels supported by uprights and it should be noted that there are ladies' and gentlemen's bicycles "made for two" . . .In 1900 it may interest you to note that nearly 6,000 trips were made, this railway going all day long. Open free from 9.00 to 6.30.'

The usual arrangements were made for sea bathing, the Company hiring bathing

The Town Hall and Town Quay from the Haven Bridge, Great Yarmouth. Mr Walters wrote in 1893 that 'the view of the shipping along the quay, the Town Hall &c., is most charming, and one not readily forgotten.' A small coastal steamer is seen unloading general cargo which is being transferred into railway wagons on the quayside

machines identified by the labels 'Bass & Co', seven for the ladies and fourteen for the men, segregated south and north respectively of the Britannia Pier. Costumes, drawers and towels were supplied. A feature of the earlier trips to Yarmouth was the hiring of twenty donkeys for free use by women and children during the day. The Bass donkeys were distinguished by red, white and blue rosettes for easy identification.

The *Yarmouth Independent* wrote on 22 July 1905: 'Like all other places the Police Station was "Free to Bass" but it was the one place where Bass could not be found, the conduct

Bass Special No.10 arrived at Great Yarmouth at 10.10am on Friday, 23 July 1909, the passengers including manual and office workers from the Stables and Shobnall. As usual, Mr Simnett is perched on his ladder to record the arrivals. An earlier arrival stands at the adjacent platform, but it is evident that no time has been lost in releasing the locomotives of both trains prior to removing the carriages to the sidings.

of the representatives of that honourable name being excellent.'

It was on the Yarmouth trip of 1901 that there occurred the one serious accident directly associated with the Bass railway trains. The *Burton Daily Mail* of Saturday, 15 June 1901 reported that the severely mutilated body of a man was found on the railway line at Holwell Sidings, about two and a half miles on the Nottingham side of Melton Mowbray. In his possession was Bass Ticket No.2735, from which it was assumed that he had fallen from Train No.9 on the return journey from Yarmouth, although it was thought possible that he was on the last train, No.16. Police who attended the scene found on the body two half-pennies, a photograph, a bottle of whisky, a railway ticket and the Bass Trip ticket. He was named as John Bullen, 136 Station Street. He was a maltster with Messrs Bass & Co.

An inquest into the death was held at Asfordby on Friday, 21 June. The evidence was conflicting, but there was a suggestion that there had been a row in the carriage in which the victim had travelled. The Coroner's jury reached their verdict: 'The deceased met his death by falling from a train, but how he came to fall there was not sufficient evidence to show.'

On a less serious note it is said that on at least one trip several men of the visiting party made straight for the nearest public house in Great Yarmouth and stayed there for the rest of the day. But there were others who did not get so far. They had clubbed together to buy their own cask of beer in Burton and were so much the worse for wear on reaching Yarmouth that they were simply shunted into the sidings and never left the train.

Train Arrangements.

The Route Map at the back of this Sheet will enable you to follow the Journey throughout.

ALL THE TRAINS will Start from Burton Railway Station (St. Paul's side Platform) —for View see page 10—and, on returning, from Vauxhall Station, Yarmouth—for View see page 16.

NOTE.—**HAVE YOUR TICKETS READY.**—All persons will be required to show their Railway Ticket at the Doors at the Main Entrance, and at the Barriers at the top of the steps, at Burton Station, and none but Excursionists travelling by these Trains will be allowed upon the Platforms. The Tickets will also be examined at the Platform Barriers at Yarmouth, before leaving for Burton, and must be given up at the Barriers at Burton Station AT NIGHT. Persons using the Barton and Walton and Branstone Train, and the Tutbury Local Special, will, of course, show their Tickets in the morning, and give them up at night when alighting at their *own* Station. See page 9.

The Foremen and Men employed in the Various Departments, with their Wives and all others for whom they have obtained Tickets, must travel by their OWN Train—both going and returning—as under:—

No. of Train.	DEPARTMENT, &c.	OUTWARD JOURNEY.		RETURN JOURNEY.	
		Depart Burton.	Arrive Yarmouth.	Depart Yarmouth.	Arrive Burton.
		A.M.	A.M	P.M.	A.M.
1	Mr. Ollis—Blacksmiths, Bricklayers, Coppersmiths, Plumbers, and Wheelwrights	3.45	8.20	7.35	12.15
2	Mr. Ollis—Fitters and Joiners	3.55	8.35	7.45	12.20
3	New Brewery Mr. Ollis—Painters, Saxby	4.5	8.45	7.55	12.30
4	Old Brewery Mr. J. Clubb—Shobnall Mr. Ollis—Tailors, Cloggers, and Wireworkers	4.15	8.50	8.5	12.50
5	Mr. J. Clubb—Middle Yard except Shobnall Mr. Ollis—Excavators and Platelayers,	4.25	9.0	8.15	12.55
6	Mr. R. W. Clubb—Steam Cooperage Mr. Elson Gas Works, and Electric Works	4.35	9.25	8.25	1.5
7	Mr. R. W. Clubb—Repairing Cooperage	4.45	9.35	8.35	1.10
8	Grain Department	5.0	9.45	8.45	1.20
9	Mr. Williamson—Railway Department	5.10	10.0	8.55	1.30
10	Mr. Hodgkinson—Stables Mr. Oliver Mr. Ollis—Office and Shobnall	5.20	10.10	9.0	1.35
11	The Estate, Farm, Gardens and Stables, at Rangemore, and at Byrkley, &c. This Train ONLY will take up and set down at BARTON and WALTON and at BRANSTONE	5.30	10.20	9.15	1.50
12	Middle Brewery Local Special from Tutbury, &c.	5.40	10.30	9.25	1.55
13	The Customers This Train will take up and set down Customers at REPTON and WILLINGTON.	5.50	10.40	9.35	2.10
14	Clerks This Train will take up and set down Passengers at REPTON and WILLINGTON.	6.0	10.50	9.45	2.25
15	Mr. Walters and Friends DERBY PASSENGERS must travel by this Train between Burton and Yarmouth BOTH WAYS.	6.10	10.55	9.55	2.35

Placards will be found affixed to each Train, both at Burton and at Yarmouth, plainly indicating the number of the Train. There will also be Boards—giving the number of each Train—placed on the Indicator at the bottom of the Steps leading to the Platform (to the **Right** hand) at Burton.—Prominent Notices will also be found on the Platforms at Yarmouth.

SPECIAL NOTE.—Third Class Passengers must travel 8 in each Compartment, and, where necessary, 5 on each side—the same as ordinary passengers—and this must be strictly carried out in all the Trains.

VERY URGENT.—It is imperative that all persons should Travel both Ways by their Own Train, and most urgently does this apply to the Earlier Trains on the Return Journey. The Great Eastern Railway Company are most particular about you travelling by your own Train, and seeing Your Ticket, so be fully prepared at Yarmouth at night.

☞ Remember to bring ALL your Railway Tickets, and have them ready at Burton and at Yarmouth Stations.

The Special Train arrangements for Great Yarmouth, Friday, 23 July 1909.

Scarborough

Scarborough on a wet day is infinitely worse than the bottle of flat beer.

Scarborough Post, Friday, 17 June 1898

SCARBOROUGH was the most attractive destination for the Bass Trips from the scenic point of view. The good sandy beaches of the North and South Bays were separated by the headland, topped by the castle ruins overlooking the old town and harbour on the south side. Although the railway had introduced the mass holiday trippers in the nineteenth century there was still something of the refinement and gentility of the spa which had first brought the town to the attention of the wider public, but there were also sufficient facilities to cope with the demands of the huge Bass excursions. Here, as at the other destinations, the local railway company agreed that no other excursion would be run to the resort on the same day as the Bass Specials. Indeed it would be hard to imagine there being sufficient room on the local lines for any other such traffic.

The first Bass trip to the Yorkshire coast was in 1881, but the return visit was not until 1890

Scarborough was scenically the most interesting of the places visited by Bass, with its two bays separated by the headland surmounted by the remains of the castle. This view of South Bay, its sandy beach largely covered by the incoming tide, contains the main elements of the resort. The old town nestles beneath the castle, close to the harbour on the right. Cheap cafes line the sea front, sailing boats await customers, and horses are dragging bathing machines into the deeper water. Lines of towels can be seen drying by the nearest machines. On the left is the Grand Hotel, which William Walters used as his operations base and for the official dinners for Agency Staff and other invited guests on Bass Trip days. North Yorkshire County Library.

York Station, looking south along Platform 4, on an unusally quiet afternoon. In the original photograph a solitary figure can be seen beneath the station clock. The station was a scene of frenzied activity when the Bass Specials to Scarborough arrived, each train being allowed ten minutes while engines were changed and refreshments obtained.

and thereafter at four yearly intervals until 1914. The journey from Burton was 136 miles and was usually accomplished in about three and three-quarter hours. There was a break at York in both directions where, in 1910, there was such a rush for the refreshment facilities that five hundred cups and saucers were carried onto the trains, completely exhausting the stock of crockery on York station. It was understandable, then, that the handbook requested the excursionists to place all crockery carefully on the racks in their compartments.

North of York, the Bass Specials ran on to the tracks of the North Eastern Railway, whose engines were exchanged with the Midland's during the ten-minute break at York. In 1906 it was announced that the Midland engines would work the Specials right through, under the guidance of NER pilotmen. In 1910, when it seemed that industrial action might prevent the running of the excursions on the NER, Mr Walters rose to the challenge by arranging for fifteen Midland drivers to be sent to York on

the previous day, to learn the signals from there to Scarborough, in case there were insufficient local men available. In the event the dispute was resolved in time for normal running, which he had felt confident would happen all along. One of the worst delays experienced by the Bass Specials happened on the homeward journey in 1902, when the first train was 48 minutes late, so delaying all the rest, including No.6 train which left a carriage at Masborough with a hot axle box. The *Burton Daily Mail* described the delays as 'unprecedented'.

Entertainments at Scarborough included concerts and other amusements in the Spa and the Aquarium, bathing machines, free donkeys (marked with coloured Rosettes) for the use of women and children, while the Corporation allowed the use of the Cliff Tramways free for the day on production of the railway ticket. Among the more unusual entertainments laid on were daylight firework displays, organised by Messrs C.T.Brock & Co. These had been a disappointment in 1890 because of rough

Bass Special No.4 has just arrived at Scarborough on Friday, 22 July 1910, carrying people from the New Brewery and the Joiners' Department. It is 7.55am and thirteen hours of enjoyment lies ahead of them before the return journey.

inshore winds, but in 1894 the crowds were able to enjoy pyrotechnic tableaux featuring the *Flags of the Nations* and other fluttering objects, the *Japanese Fat Woman, Descent of the Cow that jumped over the Moon* and the *Finale*, described as the *Animated Olla Podrida, human, quadrupedal, ornithological, piscine and reptilian*. Trips to sea were available in 1890 and 1894 using the steamers *Nunthorpe* and *Cleveland*, chartered from the NER. In 1881 the *Scarborough* was brought specially from Gainsborough to supplement the sea-trips. She was used again in 1894 and 1898, on the latter occasion being joined by the *Atalanta*.

A sandcastle building competition organised for children on Scarborough's South Beach, about 1900. At high tide the beach would be swept clean once again. Dominating the scene on the cliff top is the Grand Hotel, where William Walters made his headquarters. From here he superintended the activities, hosting the dinner for guests of Messrs Bass & Co, and providing assistance to trippers, such as the replacement of lost tickets before the journey home. In 1890 only six people out of six thousand lost their tickets.   Postcard, Author's collection.

High tide but a calm sea, enabling the bathing machines to remain on the beach.

It was at Scarborough that the only other fatality associated with the Bass Trips occurred, an incident not connected with the trains and seemingly owing much to bad luck and misjudgement by several persons.

The *Burton Daily Mail* of Saturday, 18 June 1898 headlined its report 'The Scarborough Fatality' and went on: 'Joseph Tomlinson (58) Bricklayer's labourer, one of Bass's colossal trip to Scarborough, died yesterday at Scarborough Hospital as a result of injuries received earlier

in the day. William Gledhill, steam packet manager of Gainsborough, was going to see Mr Walters at the Grand Hotel, when he noticed a man asleep on a portable crane in a dangerous position on the East Pier. He called two policemen's attention to him. They assisted him off the platform, put him on his feet and left hold. Instead of him going straight he took a roll and knocked against the deceased, who was standing at the edge of the pier. Tomlinson fell over into the harbour head first, a distance

Modern motor charabancs were available at reasonable prices for trips into the surrounding countryside. Twenty-eight people, including the driver, are about to set off in 1914, bound perhaps for Hayburn Wyke, Forge Valley or Filey.

Train No.6 in 1910, with passengers from the Old Brewery and Shobnall pouring from the open carriage doors. At least one stone jar of beer has survived the journey.

of 10 or 12 feet. The man who knocked the deceased over was a stranger. He was apparently drunk. Tomlinson suffered severe head injuries, both arms fractured and shock. He died later. Verdict: "Accidental Death".'

The severity of Tomlinson's injuries had been caused when he hit some stone steps. Several of his friends and relatives were on the trip; his son-in-law, Edward Slater, was informed of the accident at 4pm, and was

requested to be present at the inquest a week later, in order to provide formal identification.

Considering that over the years some 256,000 trippers took part in the Bass Trips, the accident record was remarkably good; only the Yarmouth fatality actually occurred on the train journey. Perhaps it was with good reason that Mr Walters concluded his handbooks by suggesting that 'one and all be thankful to the Almighty for so mercifully preserving us in

Sea trips were features of the Bass visits to Scarborough. A regular favourite was the paddle steamer Scarborough, *licensed for 300 passengers, seen quietly moored alongside the lighthouse. The funnel of a second vessel can be seen to the right, while one of the local fishing boats is moored on the left.* North Yorkshire County Library.

safety during the very many long years of these Excursions.' But it was also a tribute to the careful and detailed planning that went into every aspect of the excursions which left very little to chance. As a final precaution it was the practice for many years to insist that the trippers purchase an insurance ticket to cover any eventuality on the day of the excursion.

The Last Bass Trip

The last Bass Trip ran on Friday, 24 July 1914, when fourteen trains arrived at the special excursion station at Scarborough, bringing about 8,000 trippers. All trains arrived ten minutes ahead of their scheduled times, using

Midland locomotives throughout the journey. The handbook for this excursion has been reprinted by the Bass Museum and is well worth a close study. It reveals a considerable decline in the attractions available free to the Bass excursionists and the day's programme occupies only a half-page in the book. Free admission was granted to the Spa, where refreshments and shelter were available, with a free programme of music. Similar facilities, including a free variety show, were available at the People's Palace and Aquarium, while there was free travel throughout the day on the two cliff tramways connecting the town with the beaches. But that was all. Anything else had to be paid for by the individual trippers, although cheap concessions had been negotiated. The sea trips were still available, using the steamers *Scarborough* and *Cambria*, at one shilling for longer trips or sixpence for shorter trips. The handbook itself, with relatively few illustrations and only a little different to the previous issue, reflected an apparent need for economy on the part of the organisers. Indeed, Mr Walters had, for the past few years, been given clear instructions that restraint must be exercised and that the days of open-handed expenditure were over.

It is not known how the trippers reacted to the cut-back in their free entertainment, but within a very short while they would have other, more serious matters to occupy their minds. The *Burton Daily Mail* on Saturday, 25 July 1914 carried its usual report of the Bass Trip. Elsewhere in the same issue was a short paragraph reporting the "Continental Crisis" in which the principal actors were Austria, Serbia, Germany and Russia. Although this must have seemed a remote event, just two weeks later Britain was at war with Germany.

Preparations for the coming conflict had been in hand for several years. The Royal Navy was the largest in the world and had some of the most modern fighting vessels available to it. During the summer season parts of the fleet had been visiting major seaside resorts, to show the public something of the results of public expenditure on their behalf. On the occasion of the Bass visit to Scarborough in 1914 several Royal Navy ships were anchored offshore. Local boatmen were not slow to take the opportunity to earn a few pence by ferrying out trippers, half a dozen at a time, to get a closer view of the fleet. However, one group of Burtonians got rather closer to the fleet than they had anticipated. The 'hero' (or villain) of the piece was a whitesmith, known to his workmates as Cakey. He was a hard-working man, but one who loved to indulge in practical jokes.

Several of the little boats loaded up and put to sea. When they were some distance out, someone asked, "Where's Cakey?" He was in another boat. Shouting, "Here I am!" he stood on the gunwhale of his boat and dived into

The first of the Bass pin-up girls, Scarborough 1906. Beyond her parasol can be seen some of the scenic attractions of the resort.

the sea, fully clothed. He was a powerful swimmer and cut a good figure as he swam towards the first boat. Reaching it, he put a hand on the side, whereupon the occupants shouted, "You ainna comin' in here!" "No," he said, "You're coming in with me!" and he pulled the boat over, spilling the occupants into the water. Whether or not any could swim had not entered into the calculation. Fortunately they were near a man-of-war, from where the antics had been observed. A boat was lowered and the unfortunates were rescued without loss. They were of course soaked, so their clothes were taken and dried, while they were dressed up as sailors. They all had a good time on board, thanks to Cakey!

Trips and Trippers

THE employees of Messrs Bass, Ratcliff & Gretton were left in no doubt as to the source of funding for their excursions. At the end of the handbook Mr Walters never failed to remind his passengers of the source of their pleasure: 'I am sure that all of you again sincerely wish to thank the Directors for their kindness in providing this outing for you and your families — an outing which many of you could not otherwise possibly enjoy.'

The Trips were funded by the Company Directors from the petty cash account. The details are available from 1901 and are listed in *Table 2*, although it should be noted that these figures are slightly at variance with those recorded in the Directors' Minutes. For example, it was stated in the minutes that the costs of the Scarborough Trips in 1906 and 1910 were £2,905 and £1,639 respectively, but shown in the accounts as £3,222 and £1,873. From 1910 to the end there is a sharp drop in the expenditure on these outings. This reflected several factors, including a change in management following the death of Lord Burton in 1909, a deterioration in trading conditions for the brewing industry, and also a feeling that the scale of the Bass excursions was getting out of hand. It was decided to cut back on the expenditure involved, as shown in resolutions contained in the Directors' minutes.

At their meeting on 21 February 1910 it was resolved: That the date of the Workmen's Excursion be fixed for Friday, 22 July, and the destination Scarborough. The expenses in connection with this excursion to be reduced as near £2,300 as possible. Tickets to outsiders to be raised. The cost of the excursion books to be reduced to £300 if possible.

The Excursion Handbooks

Starting with the first excursion in 1865, the Bass trippers were issued with printed instructions concerning the running of the trains and general notes of guidance about their expected behaviour. In 1893 the first handbook was produced, for Great Yarmouth. The booklet measured 7¼ x 9¾in (186 x 249mm), which remained the standard size until

1900. It contained full details of the train times, the day's programme of entertainments and seven pages of information about the journey and places of interest in Yarmouth. Along with the handbook

Michael Arthur Bass, 1st Lord Burton, 1837-1909. He had actively encouraged the running of the Bass Trips since their inception in 1865. His death in 1909 severed the Bass family link with the brewing company and the Directors took the opportunity to scale down the expenditure on the Trips, which were funded from their own petty cash account.

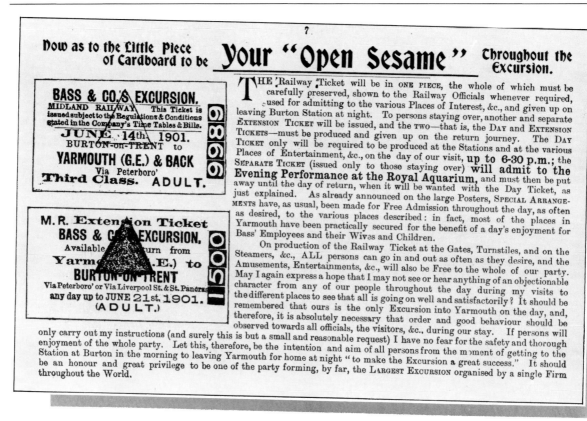

7.

Now as to the Little Piece of Cardboard to be Your "Open Sesame" Throughout the Excursion.

THE Railway Ticket will be in ONE PIECE, the whole of which must be carefully preserved, shown to the Railway Officials whenever required, used for admitting to the various Places of Interest, &c., and given up on leaving Burton Station at night. To persons staying over, another and separate EXTENSION TICKET will be issued, and the TWO—that is, the DAY and EXTENSION TICKETS—must be produced and given up on the return journey. The DAY TICKET only will be required to be produced at the Stations and at the various Places of Entertainment, &c., on the day of our visit, up to 6-30 p.m.; the SEPARATE TICKET (issued only to those staying over) will admit to the Evening Performance at the Royal Aquarium, and must then be put away until the day of return, when it will be wanted with the Day Ticket, as just explained. As already announced on the large Posters, SPECIAL ARRANGEMENTS have, as usual, been made for Free Admission throughout the day, as often as desired, to the various places described: in fact, most of the places in Yarmouth have been practically secured for the benefit of a day's enjoyment for Bass' Employees and their Wives and Children.

On production of the Railway Ticket at the Gates, Turnstiles, and on the Steamers, &c., ALL persons can go in and out as often as they desire, and the Amusements, Entertainments, &c., will also be Free to the whole of our party. May I again express a hope that I may not see or hear anything of an objectionable character from any of our people throughout the day during my visits to the different places to see that all is going on well and satisfactorily? It should be remembered that ours is the only Excursion into Yarmouth on the day, and, therefore, it is absolutely necessary that order and good behaviour should be observed towards all officials, the visitors, &c., during our stay. If persons will only carry out my instructions (and surely this is but a small and reasonable request) I have no fear for the safety and thorough enjoyment of the whole party. Let this, therefore, be the intention and aim of all persons from the moment of getting to the Station at Burton in the morning to leaving Yarmouth for home at night "to make the Excursion a great success." It should be an honour and great privilege to be one of the party forming, by far, the LARGEST EXCURSION organised by a single Firm throughout the World.

Great Yarmouth 1901. Instructions about the use of the railway tickets (which bore the red Bass triangle) as issued by William Walters in the handbook.

the trippers were also given a copy of *The Popular Guide to Yarmouth,* which was illustrated and contained a town plan which had been specially printed for the trip to enable the points of interest to be easily located. In the following year the booklet for Scarborough contained its own photographs, many of which were specially taken for the publication, which became more elaborate and sophisticated over the years.

Colour was used for the booklet covers and in 1902 a specially designed cover, prepared by Major W. Boden, the Bass Manager at Sheffield, depicted a view of the old lighthouse at Scarborough and the label of a bottle of Bass's Pale Ale. Boden also provided an interesting cover for the Liverpool booklet of 1903, incorporating a picture of the RMS *Lucania* in dock and three bottles of Bass's ales. However, this handbook was never issued because of a last-minute change in destination, the result of an outbreak of smallpox in Liverpool. A replacement guide for Blackpool was hastily cobbled together, containing several pages of last-minute information stuck into the booklet after printing. The production was a remarkable achievement in a very short time, but its size was only forty-four pages, compared with 102 for Scarborough in 1902 and ninety-six pages in the abandoned booklet for Liverpool. The Liverpool effort was not totally in vain, because much of it was simply reprinted in the following year. However, Mr Walters was left with some 10,000 copies of the 1903 booklet, now useless, on his hands.

The enforced cut in expenditure on the trip handbook is clear from 1910. The number of illustrations was drastically reduced and the pictures were printed on a limited number of pages only. Although the printed words were as comprehensive as ever, much of the exuberance and style of the earlier volumes had been lost, matching the reduced entertainments which were on offer to the trippers at the resorts.

The Bass Trippers

The first Bass Trip of 1865 was given as a treat to the company's workmen only, marshalled on to the trains under their foremen. On later Trips they were allowed to bring wives and children, on payment of the rail fare for the extra guests. Over the years the scope of the Trips became larger and invitations were issued to customers of the firm, who travelled in the later trains, which even made stops at neighbouring stations such as Willington and Derby in order to accommodate them. Once equipped with the Bass Excursion ticket, all were entitled to the entertainments offered free or at concessionary rates, many taking advantage of the extension tickets to enjoy longer stays at the resorts. The composition of the trippers varied over the years. Writing in the Yarmouth handbook of 1905 Mr Walters said that the number of children on the trips was usually about five hundred. However, in 1903 the *Burton Daily Mail* had said that the Blackpool trippers that year comprised 3,500

Burton upon Trent Corporation tramcars, Nos.1 and 2, specially posed at the foot of Bearwood Hill Road, soon after the opening of services in 1903. Tramcars were run early in the morning and late at night to connect with the Bass special trains. In 1914 Mr Walters felt obliged to remind his excursionists to make use of the facilities, otherwise they would be withdrawn. A.T.Moss.

Bass Trips: Costs 1901-1914
Table 2

		Total Cost	of which is Stationery Dept
1901	Yarmouth	£3,518	£490
1902	Scarborough	£3,637	£556
1903	Blackpool	£3,317	£623
1904	Liverpool	£3,102	£529
1905	Yarmouth	£3,619	£518
1906	Scarborough	£3,222	£617
1907	Blackpool	£3,417	£597
1908	Liverpool	£2,484	£441
1909	Yarmouth	£3,153	£581
1910	Scarborough	£1,873	£13
1911	Blackpool	£2,002	£14
1912	Liverpool	£1,761	£13
1913	Yarmouth	£2,109	*
1914	Scarborough	£1,837	†

* Less than £1
†Not given
Costs 'not including value of the men's time.'
Source: Balance Sheets, Bass, Ratcliff & Gretton, Petty Cash Accounts.

men, 3,000 women and 3,000 children, perhaps an exceptional number on that occasion.

In the early days it was the practice to take a sounding of the workmen to decide the destination for the Trip, which produced separate excursions on three occasions. As the Trips became larger it was more practicable to concentrate the efforts on one destination at a time, which of course strengthened the negotiating hand of Mr Walters with the railways and the seaside concessionaries. The last year in which it is known that a choice

The Burton Volunteer Band, supported by Lord Burton, played regularly at the resorts on Trip days. Their programme for Friday, 16 June 1899 comprised two concerts at St George's Hall, Liverpool.

could be exercised was in 1891, when at a meeting of the Board of Directors on 29 June it was minuted that:

'Liverpool 1,245
London 719
Scarborough 345

It was resolved that the excursion be to Liverpool on Friday the 14 August.'

One group of staff at the Bass Offices in Burton upon Trent was unable to participate in the annual Trips. These were the staff who handled the various Agency accounts, which at this time were closed on 30 June, the balance work involving overtime in June and July. They were compensated with their own outing arranged by the Traffic Office. There was an excursion booklet which gave details of the day's activities. A typical journey started with

Burton and Ashby Light Railways trams ran into Burton between 1906 and 1927. This car is standing at Newhall, during a test run over the route before opening. Arrangements were made with the tramway for special cars to be run to connect with the Bass excursion trains. A.T.Moss.

breakfast on a special dining saloon attached to a service train for Derby and through to Bakewell or Rowsley, where they were met by horse-drawn brakes for a scenic tour, interrupted by a luncheon stop at a suitable hostelry. Visits were made to such attractions as Haddon Hall or Chatsworth, while the day was rounded off with a multiple course dinner at Matlock, before the return by rail to Burton.

Gratuities

It was the practice of Messrs Bass, Ratcliff & Gretton, in line with the other brewers in Burton, to give the workmen their day's wages

and a gratuity, which remained unchanged for many years at 2s 6d (*12½p*) for men and 5s (*25p*) for foremen. By 1908 the gratuities had been increased, so that boys received 2s 6d, and the men 5s each, while 'the more responsible company servants,' in other words Heads of Departments and office staff, received one guinea and a first-class ticket. When it is considered that the average wage of the workmen was just over £1 a week, it is clear that the gratuity was a generous sum which would have eased the financial strains of the day trip. On the last page of a booklet for the 1909 Yarmouth Trip, preserved at the Bass

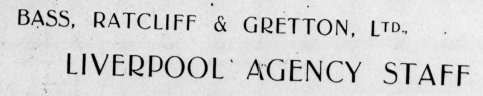

The Liverpool Agency organised annual staff outings, usually hiring private dining saloons which were attached to regular trains of the Midland Railway. In 1906 they went to Bakewell, while the following year they joined the main Bass Trip to Blackpool. They produced their own booklets, which contained a parody of William Walters' words of warning and caution. His reaction is not known!

Bass, Ratcliff & Gretton Ltd maintained agencies in several major cities around the country. Their staff were usually invited to join the Bass Trips, although sometimes it was more convenient for them to run their own outings. The staff of the Liverpool agency are seen posed outside the St James' Street office, but by the time the picture had been published in the 1899 handbook they had moved to more substantial premises in Fenwick Street.

Museum, is a handwritten entry in pencil recording the expenses of an anonymous tripper, probably a juvenile, which shows just how far half-a-crown (*12½p*) could stretch at that time.

It notes:

Breakfast 5d
Dinner 3d
Tea 6d
Tram 1d
Narners (?) 1d
Sweet 4d + 1
Nell (?) 6½d
Pier 1d

This amounted to 2s 4½d and seemed to have ensured a reasonable day out. The identity of 'Nell' remains a mystery, although she was the most expensive item on the list!

End of the Bass Trips

IT IS possible that the advent of World War One simply speeded the end of the Bass Trips. The financing of the Trips was becoming less easy in the later years, the enthusiasm of the Directors was diminishing and the actual size of the excursions was gradually falling. The problems of the wartime economy enabled them to bow out of the railway excursions with a good grace, while continuing some of the benefits for the workforce. There are two items in the minutes of the Board of Directors of Messrs Bass, Ratcliff & Gretton which show precisely how and why the Bass Trips were stopped. These are:

'8 March 1915:

Resolved: That the Workmen's Excursion be discontinued for the present year on account of the difficulties of the Railway Company occasioned by the war with Germany.'

'21 June 1915:

Resolved: That the Trip be abandoned this year, but in its place each employee have a Saturday Holiday. Those on the wages list to receive the half-day's wages (piece workmen as per rate formerly paid) and a gift of 2/6d excepting the boys of under 21 years of age, who are to receive 2/-s. Foremen to receive 5/-s, the same gratuity as when there was a trip.'

The same arrangements were made in 1916, 1917 and 1918, with a half-day's holiday granted in lieu of a Trip, but after that the Minutes make no further reference to the Excursion or the holiday. A further

New Brighton in 1912, the last year that the Bass Trips visited Liverpool. The huge liner Lusitania *is dwarfed by the New Brighton Tower as the ship enters the Mersey, escorted by a tug boat. The outbreak of war stopped the Trips in 1915, and in the same year the* Lusitania *was sunk by a German torpedo in the Atlantic. By 1920 the Tower had disappeared for scrap.*
Liverpool City Libraries.

Burton Station just before demolition work in 1971. William Walters used a similar view in some of the Trip handbooks, with a plea that on the return to Burton the trippers should go 'up the steps and quietly home.'   A.T.M.

The British Empire Exhibition, 1924. The coal mine display, surrounded by various items of funfair equipment.   There were only sufficient visitors from Bass and other parties at Burton to fill two special excursion trains.
Greater London Photograph Library.

contributory factor was the retirement of Mr Walters from the Company after fifty years' service on 31 December 1915. He was granted a retiring allowance of £425 per annum, which he was able to enjoy until his death in 1923. There is a curious feature concerning Mr Walters' retirement. Although he had always welcomed publicity connected with the Company, he requested that the usual presentation in the Board Room, attended by heads of Department at Burton and of the various Agencies, with coverage by the Press, be waived. A sum of £75 7s 0d had been collected as a testimonial from his colleagues. This was

Mobilisation 1914. World War One broke out just a few days after the Bass Trip to Scarborough, although there was no apparent connection between the two events. Men of the 6th North Staffordshire Regiment are seen marching with their band through Burton after enlistment. Only a few weeks before, some of them would have tramped through the same streets in the early hours to take their places on the Bass Specials to Scarborough.   A.T.Moss.

used to purchase a gold engraved cigar case, at the value of £24 4s 6d, which was sent to his home in Alexandra Road, Winshill, along with a cheque for the balance of £47 2s 6d on 26 February 1916.

After the war, the brewing companies, in common with many other major industries, were faced with the necessity for stringent economy. Luxuries such as works outings were no longer possible; indeed, in 1922 the workers' wages were reduced by two shillings a week. In the post-war world attitudes in industry had undergone a revolution. The kind of paternalism expressed in the organisation of mass company outings was becoming less acceptable, while new forms of holiday habits

were beginning to emerge, in part associated with developments in road transport. The motor coach was beginning to make inroads into markets which were once the monopoly of the railways, giving more flexibility and greater choice of destinations.

The Last Trip of All

Memories of the old Bass Trips were revived briefly in 1924, when on Saturday, 23 June, four trains set out from Burton upon Trent in the early hours of the morning, carrying two thousand people on a day trip to London to visit the British Empire Exhibition at Wembley. But only two trains were chartered

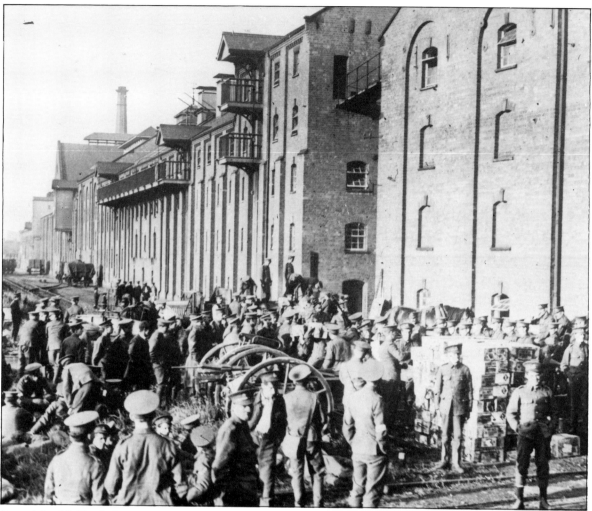

Men of the 6th North Staffordshire Regiment unloading provisions outside their temporary billets at Peach's maltings, Burton.

on behalf of the Bass employees, who had to pay their own way. The first train, which left Burton at 3.45am and arrived at Wembley at 7am, was chartered by the Junior Imperial League and had started out from Uttoxeter to pick up some of its five hundred passengers in the country districts. The two Bass trains, with a total of a thousand passengers, left at 4.40am and 5.15am, followed by the fourth train chartered on behalf of Messrs James Eadie. The trains went straight to Wembley station on the former L&NWR line, but they were only four out of a dozen trains carrying visitors on that day, drawn from Nottingham, Manchester and London. The attractions included Colonial and industrial exhibits and a large pleasure fair. The Junior Imperial League train returned from St Pancras at 10pm reaching Burton at 1am. The Bass trains, by contrast, came back from Wembley.

The *Burton Daily Mail* of Monday, 25 June 1924 described the homeward journey: 'Close on a dozen excursion trains left Wembley Station between half-past ten and midnight. Before these, two heavily loaded trains steamed out London-bound. They relieved the congestion somewhat, but still each of the platforms was thronged, and a continuing stream of returning revellers flowed down the stairs.

'The shouts of "Bass's Burton, this way," which greeted all as they came down the stairs helped the Burtonians sort themselves out and they stood in knots talking excitedly as they compared notes and discussed the experiences of the day.

'The second of the Burton trains was the last on the list, and it left Wembley to the peace and quiet of a Sunday morning. The trains did all that could be required in the way of speed, and a few minutes before 3 o'clock the last "battalion" of weary Burtonians was rushed into the hometown.'

But the excursion of 1924 was far removed in time and scale from the huge Bass Trips held before World War One. Gone were the days when, as in 1907, Mr Walters could remind his customers on the Blackpool Trip: 'It should be an honour and a privilege to be one of the party forming, by far, the LARGEST EXCURSION organised by a single firm throughout the world.'

Mobilisation day 1914. Horses provided the main means of transport and haulage in World War One and on mobilisation in August 1914 those owned by the Bass Brewery were 'called up' and paraded for inspection in Guild Street. Paralysis of local transport was threatened by the action.
                                                                A.T.Moss.

William Walters' final words in the Scarborough handbook for 1914 were the last he would address to the Bass trippers. Although the outbreak of war brought an immediate end to the Trips, it is evident that they were becoming an embarrassment to the Company's Directors, who were probably grateful for the excuse to finish the excursions.

40

Final Reminders.

"SCARBOROUGH, July 24th, 1914."

NO doubt you have all got this well off by heart, but there are other points to be kept well to the front, and it is to this end that each adult is presented with a copy of this Handbook. In it I have set forth the particulars of the various Amusements, &c., and the Directors hope that full advantage will be taken by ALL OUR EMPLOYEES AND THEIR FAMILIES of every concession extended to us.

I hope this Handbook will be found a helpful and welcome companion on the day of the Excursion, as I have tried to make it useful. I trust that every Employee, and everyone else going with us, will again cheerfully display that spirit of good fellowship which has always characterised Bass' outings, and that the general behaviour will be of the same high standard as formerly, not only for individual reputation and comfort, but for the credit of BASS, RATCLIFF, AND GRETTON, LIMITED.

No needless regulations have been made, and the few which do exist EXIST ONLY THAT THE COMFORT OF EVERYBODY MAY BE ASSURED. Don't forget to carefully look out YOUR OWN TRAIN, and, when found, see that you travel by it EACH WAY. Avoid any crowding at the Platforms, Landing Stages, or Piers. Wait until the gangways are securely fixed.

In conclusion, I am sure that all of you again sincerely wish to thank the Directors for their kindness in providing this outing for you and your families—an outing which many of you could not otherwise possibly enjoy—and let one and all be thankful to the Almighty for so mercifully preserving us in safety during the very many long years of these Excursions.

I hope you will all enjoy your outing, short or long, and return in safety to good old Burton.

By Order of the Directors,

WILLIAM WALTERS,

Traffic Manager.

TRESISES, PRINTERS, BURTON-ON-TRENT.

BASS & Co's
No. 15
TRAIN

THE END.